THE WORLD OF FOOD

Italy

The World of Food

Italy

by *Luigi Veronelli*

WORLD PUBLISHING
TIMES MIRROR
NEW YORK

Luigi Veronelli has dedicated himself to the enjoyable discipline of gastronomy. He is the author of nine books on food and wine, including *Il Gastronomo (The Gastronome)*, *La Cucina d'Amore (Cooking for Lovers)*, *I Vini Francesi (French Wines)*, *Il Dizionario Gastronomico (Gastronomic Dictionary)*, and *Il Vino Giusto (The Right Wine)*. Three of his books on wines and spirits—*I Cocktails (Cocktails)*, *I Vini d'Italia (The Wines of Italy)*, and *Il Gotha dei Vini del Mondo (Who's Who of the World's Wines)*— are considered standard reference works. With Luigi Carnacina he is coauthor of *Mangiare e Bere all'Italiana (Eating and Drinking Italian Style)* and *La Vera Buona Cucina Italiana (Genuine Italian Cuisine)*. Mr. Veronelli's cooking column appears in the daily newspaper *Il Giorno*.

Published by The World Publishing Company
Published simultaneously in Canada
by Nelson, Foster & Scott Ltd.

First printing–1973

ISBN 0-529-04862-0
Library of Congress catalog card number: 72-86305
Printed in the United States of America

Project Director: Peter V. Ritner
Associate Project Director and Editor-In-Chief: Richard M. Beebe
Associate Editor: Mary Lee Allingham

Creative Director and Designer: Milton Charles
Assistant to Creative Director: Terry McKee
Illustrations: Ron Le Hew

Production Manager: Bernard Kass

ACKNOWLEDGMENTS
British Consulting Editor: Katie Stewart
American Consulting Editor: Ann Seranne
Liaison Editor: Audrey Ellis
Photographs by Eric Carter (with the exception of those on pp. 16, 18, 19, 53, 111, 115)
Photographs by John Lee on pp. 16, 18, 19, 53, 111, 115

WORLD PUBLISHING
TIMES MIRROR

Contents

Glossary

agnolotti: squares or rounds of pasta which are filled; similar to ravioli.

al dente: literally, "to the tooth"; term used to describe the point at which pasta or rice is cooked; slightly resistant and underdone.

anchovies: small saltwater fish with a unique flavor, used extensively in Italian cooking. In Italy, the whole fish, either fresh or packed in oil or brine, is most commonly used. The canned fillets packed in oil may be substituted but they should be soaked for a short time in milk, warm water, or vinegar to remove excess salt before being prepared.

anellini: "little rings"; pasta which is usually served in soup.

anolini: semicircles of pasta which are filled, like tiny turnovers; generally cooked and served in stock.

antipasto: literally, "before the meal"; hors d'oeuvre or first course.

basil: an herb with a deliciously spicy and aromatic scent; used a great deal in Italy to flavor tomato sauce, salads, soups, and is essential for *pesto*. It loses much of its flavor when dried, so use fresh whenever possible.

bavette: thin rods of pasta with a semicircular cross section.

bel paese: a soft cheese, mild in flavor; may be used as a substitute for mozzarella.

borage: a rough blue-flowered herb that has the pronounced flavor of cucumber.

bouquet garni: "herb bouquet" made from several herbs tied together or placed in a small bag of washed cheesecloth for easy removal before serving. The most commonly used bouquet garni is a combination of parsley, thyme, and bay leaf, though other herbs are sometimes added or substituted.

bucatini: hollow pasta that looks like fat spaghetti with a hole; macaroni can be used as a substitute.

anellini

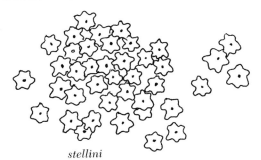

stellini

conchiglie

vermicelli

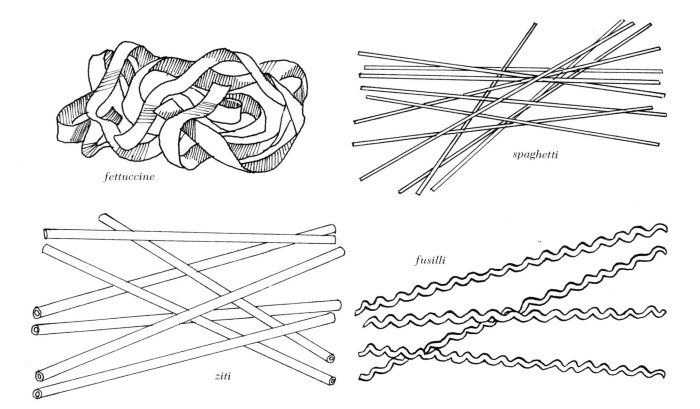

fettuccine

spaghetti

fusilli

ziti

cacio: a southern cheese; similar in taste and texture to provolone.

caciotta: a soft, fresh, rough-textured Tuscan cheese; made from whole milk, it is round and has a smooth, thin, straw-colored crust.

canneloni: large squares of pasta, cooked in boiling water, stuffed, rolled, and browned in the oven; or pasta in the form of large tubes, boiled, stuffed, and cooked in the oven.

cappelletti: "little hats"; rounds or semicircles of pasta, stuffed and rolled.

chop: to cut food into small pieces. A large knife with a triangular blade is the best tool for chopping. Rest the blade of the knife on the food, holding the point down with your left hand. Hold the handle with your right hand and with rapid up-and-down movements, chop the food, swinging the knife in an arc to reach all the food on the chopping board. This technique is interchangeable with the one described for mincing.

cinnamon: highly fragrant and sweetly aromatic spice; it is occasionally used in meat and game dishes, as well as in cakes and puddings.

codeghi: a spiced sausage with a high percentage of lean meat.

colander: a bowl-shaped utensil, usually made of metal, which has perforations permitting its use as a strainer.

conchiglie: "conch shells"; there are at least 7 sizes of this pasta; the giant shells are often grooved and served stuffed. The small ones are served in soup.

cotechino: a large round pork sausage, highly spiced, seasoned with garlic, then salted for a few days.

cuttlefish: a mollusk, similar to squid, with a central bone, a sack of "ink," and a yellowish deposit under the head. It needs careful cooking if it is to be tender. Squid may be used as a substitute.

dice: to cut food into small cubes, about ⅛ inch in size. To dice an onion or shallot, cut the vegetable in half horizontally through the root. Lay the cut side down on the chopping board. With the knife pointing toward the root end, make several vertical cuts, leaving the slices attached to the root. Then make horizontal cuts through the onion or shallot from bottom to top, still leaving the slices attached to the root. Finally, slice downward to the board at ⅛-inch intervals and the onion or shallot will fall into dice.

dried cod: must be soaked in several changes of cold water for at least 12 hours before cooking. It should have white flesh which flakes easily.

dried mushrooms: frequently used when fresh are unavailable. When buying them, look for creamy-brown color; black ones are not freshly dried and have a strong flavor and coarse texture. Soak in water to soften before using in the same manner and quantities as fresh mushrooms.

9

farfalle: "butterflies"; bow-shaped flat pasta.

fennel: an anise-flavored herb. The bulbous root-stem of the Florentine fennel is eaten both raw and cooked. Both the stalks and leaves of the wild fennel are chopped and used in stuffings.

fettuccine: "small ribbons"; egg noodles which vary in width.

fontina: a rich Piedmontese cheese, similar to Swiss Gruyère. It has small holes, is white or pale yellow, and is always used for *fonduta*.

fregula: small Sardinian *gnocchi*, made with semolina.

fusilli: a spiral, curly, spaghettilike pasta.

gnocchi: small pastalike dumplings. They may be made from flour, semolina, or potatoes, or a mixture of these. Different effects are produced in each region by using the local favorite method of cooking—boiling, frying, or baking—and serving the *gnocchi* with different sauces.

gorgonzola: a pungent, highly flavored cheese. Creamy white, with blue-green veins, gorgonzola is made from cow's milk.

herbs: the aromatic leaves of annual or perennial plants. They thrive in temperate climates and are used a great deal in Italian cooking. They give definite flavor to a dish and must be used subtly—like perfume.

knead: to work dough into a well-blended whole by repeatedly drawing it out and pressing it together with the knuckles and heel of the hand. The object in kneading is to make the dough perfectly smooth and to moisten and join all the gluten molecules. Although this end is invisible to the eye, the practiced hand will feel it because the dough becomes elastic.

lasagne: egg or plain noodles, cut in medium and wide widths.

lasagne verde: as above, colored green with spinach.

macaroni: general term for hollow or pierced pasta; the possibilities range from a macaroni no larger than spaghetti to a large tube, an inch in diameter.

manicotti: "small muff"; tube-shaped pasta. In spite of its name, it is usually cut into large flat squares and rolled around a stuffing. A commercial form of *manicotti* is a giant tube.

marjoram: a pungent and slightly bitter herb, similar to oregano. It should be used with discretion in soups, stews, meat dishes, and poultry.

mince: to chop very finely. This is best done with a large, triangular-bladed knife. Grip the handle and top of the blade with your right hand, and hold the top of the pointed tip-end with your left hand. Chop with rapid, up-and-down movements, constantly brushing

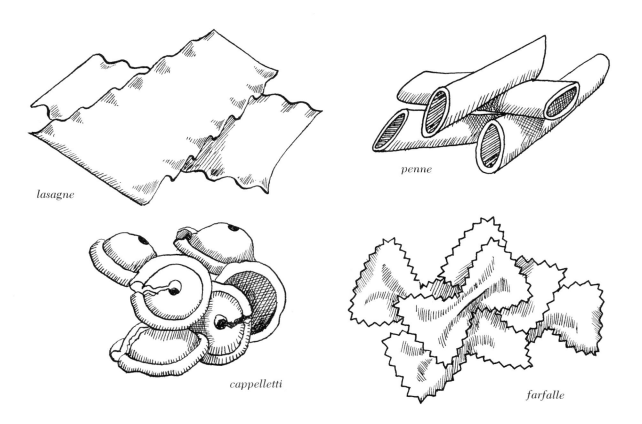

lasagne

penne

cappelletti

farfalle

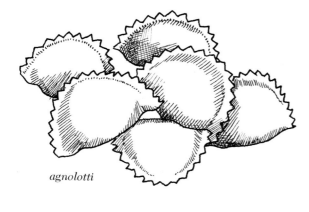

agnolotti

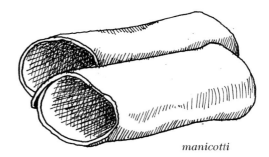

manicotti

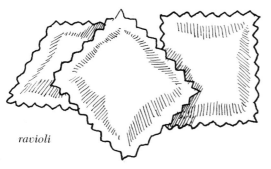

ravioli

tortellini

the ingredients into a heap in the center with the knife. This technique is interchangeable with the one described for chopping. Use the method you find more comfortable.

mortadella: Bologna sausage prepared with pork, coriander, and white wine, though there are many varieties. *Mortadella* is not cured in salt but cooked by a steam process. It was first prepared in a monastery, well before the first guild of sausage makers was formed in 1376.

mozzarella: a leavened buffaloes' milk cheese. A true mozzarella is difficult to find because buffaloes are becoming extremely rare. Mozzarella is white and rather soft, but solid enough to hold its shape. It should contain a creamy whey, which leaks out when the cheese is cut, indicating that it is fresh.

nutmeg: delicate and aromatic spice; use it sparingly but often and grind it fresh.

olive oil: oil obtained from the pulp of olives. Some of the finest olive oil in the world is produced in the Lucca region and in Sardinia. The oil from the pressed olives is refined and graded; that which rises to the top is the finest quality.

oregano: closely related to marjoram, but a more delicately flavored herb. It blends particularly well with tomato and is often used in sauces for pasta. It is also used in pork, lamb, and veal dishes. A pizza would be incomplete without oregano.

pansôti: "pot-bellied"; small squares of pasta which are filled, similar to ravioli.

parmesan: cheese made from skimmed milk which is mixed with rennet and then cooked. The resulting curds go through various processes of draining and drying, and after 6 months the cheese is sealed from the air with a black coating of burnt umber earth applied over a coating of wine or oil pressed from grape seeds. A parmesan should be pale straw-yellow, crumbly, and coarse-grained. To retain its flavor, parmesan should be bought in a piece and freshly grated every time it is needed.

pasta: generic name for the multitude of products made from flour and water; the proportions vary slightly from region to region and sometimes eggs are added. The various shapes, however, are limited only by the imagination. A particular pasta is often called for in the recipes in this book. It is the one which in size, texture, thickness, and shape is best suited to the particular sauce and method of cooking and serving. If you choose to use packaged pasta rather than make your own, you may have to make substitutions.

pasta (or noodle) machine: metal utensil, rather like a laundry mangle, used for rolling out and cutting pasta dough.

pecorino: a hard ewes' milk cheese, sometimes used as a substitute for parmesan.

pecorino sardo: Sardinian sheep's milk cheese.

penne: "pens" or "feathers"; pasta tubes cut diagonally at both ends. Macaroni may be substituted.

pesto: a paste of fresh sweet basil, parmesan cheese, garlic, and sometimes pignolia nuts, thinned with olive oil, served in soup or over pasta. A specialty of Genoa.

pignolia nuts: edible seeds of the pine nut. They are about ¼ inch long, cream-colored, and slightly oily in flavor.

polenta: a type of porridge, now made from yellow cornmeal. The staple food of Caesar's legions, it is still one of the staple foods in northern Italy. *Polenta* is eaten in several ways: hot, added to other dishes, cold, or sliced and fried.

prosciutto (Parma ham): owes its unique flavor, according to the Parmesans, to the feeding of the pigs on the whey left from making parmesan cheese, the method of curing the ham, and, most important, the dry airy climate of the hilly countryside around Parma, where thousands of salted hams are sent to be matured. Prosciutto is always eaten raw.

provolone: cheese made from buffaloes' or cows' milk, it should be eaten very fresh, when soft but firm in texture, pale yellow, and with a rich mellow flavor. Older provolone can be used for cooking.

ravioli: squares of pasta which are filled.

reduce: to rapidly boil a liquid to reduce it in quantity and concentrate its flavor.

reggiano: a hard grating cheese from Emilia-Romagna, similar to parmesan.

rice: an annual cereal grass widely cultivated in warm climates. In preparing the rice dishes in this book it is advisable to use imported Italian rice. It is large-grained and when cooked each grain should be separate and slightly resistant to the tooth. If imported rice is unavailable, use unprocessed long-grained domestic rice.

ricotta: a soft unsalted ewes' milk cheese, eaten with sugar, salt, pepper, or cinnamon, and frequently used in cooking. It should be eaten fresh, when the flavor is pungent. There are salted and smoked versions of ricotta. In cooking, cottage cheese may be substituted.

rigatoni: thick-grooved tubes of pasta, usually cut into 3-inch lengths.

rosemary: an herb with a strong, pungent aroma; the long needlelike leaves can be used fresh or dried to flavor roasts, particularly lamb.

saffron: a spice made from the stigma of autumn-flowering crocus. Saffron is used to add a subtle flavor and rich gold color to dishes. Strands of saffron are best, as they are the actual dried stigmas of the flowers.

sage: an herb with a strong, slightly bitter flavor; it marries well with rich meats but should be used with care or its taste will predominate.

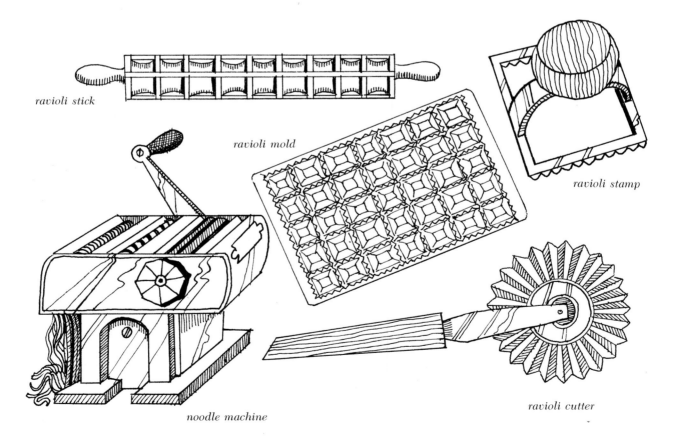

ravioli stick

ravioli mold

ravioli stamp

noodle machine

ravioli cutter

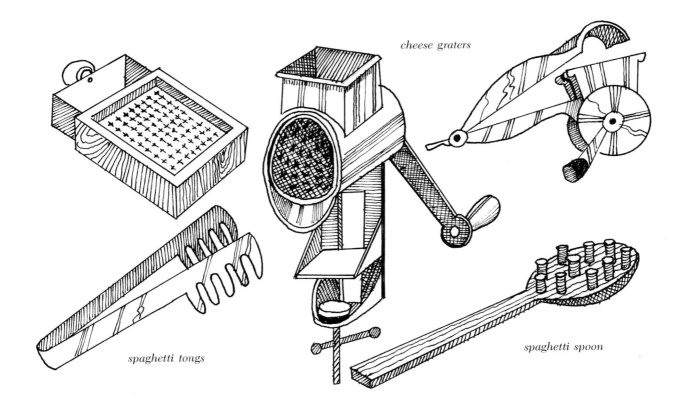

cheese graters

spaghetti tongs

spaghetti spoon

sausage: a highly seasoned finely ground mixture of pork and other meats (and sometimes cereals) that is stuffed in casings and is used either fresh or cured. Salamis—spiced sausage—gain their originality from the different methods of chopping, seasoning, salting, shaping, and maturing used in each region.

semolina: durum wheat flour used commercially for all types of pasta. It is creamy-colored, granular, and rich in protein. Semolina makes tastier pasta that also holds up better in cooking. All-purpose flour has a lower gluten content, but will do nicely for home-made pasta.

spaghetti: a solid, round rod of pasta, usually cut into lengths of about 1 foot.

spices: the roots, barks, seeds, or fruit of aromatic perennial plants.

stellini: "little stars"; pasta which is usually served in soup.

stockfish (*stoccafisso*): cod dried without salt. It is prepared by splitting, cleaning, and hanging in the open air until it is completely dry. Haddock is sometimes treated in the same manner.

stravecchio: parmesan cheese which has been aged for 3 years.

stravecchione: parmesan cheese which has been aged for 4 years.

tagliatelle: ribbon egg noodles, about ½ inch wide.

thyme: a strongly scented aromatic herb which retains its flavor well when dried.

tortelli: small semicircles of pasta which are filled with a rich stuffing.

tortellini: "small twists"; a ring-shaped pasta which is stuffed.

trenette: fine ribbon noodles.

truffles: a gnarled fungus which grows underground. Trained dogs or pigs are used to detect the truffles, which have a distinctive flavor and aroma. Truffles are sliced and used to garnish and enrich many dishes. White truffles, unique to Italy, are in fact a beige-brown color. The biggest and best white truffles come from the region of Alba in Piedmont, where they grow among the roots of oak trees.

vermicelli: "little worms"; extremely thin spaghetti, used mostly in short lengths as a garnish for soups. Sometimes 15 or 20 strands are twisted to resemble a bowknot.

zampone: highly spiced pork sausage seasoned with garlic and stuffed into the skin of a pig's foot before being boiled for hours.

ziti: "bridegrooms"; a large macaroni, a tube.

Italy

It is only in the last century that Italy has become a term of more than mere geographical convenience. Since the breakup of the Roman Empire, for more than a thousand years wars between states and against foreign invaders divided Italy into a hundred armed camps and into a fragmented collection of independent states. The topography of Italy added to the isolation between states. Great natural barriers like the Alps and the Appenines discouraged migration as much as did hostility between tribes and clans. Although unification was finally achieved in 1861, the last century has failed to wipe out deeply established regional differences in cultural and culinary traditions.

But in diversity is strength. It is precisely because it rests on a number of distinct traditions, each fiercely and jealously preserved, that Italian cuisine is extraordinarily varied and among the finest in the world. And, despite all the regional differences, there is one basic concept behind all Italian cooking: to produce simple, straightforward food with its natural flavor intact. It follows that when food is presented in such a naked manner the ingredients must be superior if it is to be more than ordinary cuisine. So, little wonder that the Italian housewife thinks nothing of shopping two or even three times a day to catch new consignments from the local gardens, for she fully realizes that good cooking begins in the market. As further evidence of their insistence on the best and freshest of ingredients, the Italians are considered extravagant when it comes to selecting raw materials. Generally, if they cannot afford the very best, they would rather go without than compromise on the quality of the dish.

If asked to describe Italian cooking, most non-Italian Americans would instantly mention such dishes as pizza, lasagne, eggplant parmigiana, spaghetti in tomato sauce, and an assortment of hot and spicy foods characterized by the heavy use of garlic. While there is nothing wrong with these foods, they are a far cry from concluding a true description of Italian cuisine. As for garlic, contrary to most thinking a great deal of Italian food is not garlicky at all—especially in northern Italy.

When speaking of spaghetti, one must remember that it is only one of the countless varieties of pasta, which in fact can be used as a basis upon which Italy can be divided between north and south. In nothern Italy pasta is usually flat and made with eggs; in the south, the pasta is tubular and generally made without eggs.

Italian vegetables are amongst the world's finest, and the main reason is that they are picked young. Their excellent tomatoes are much used in delectable soups, salads, and sauces. So are artichokes, eggplants, beans, shallots, beets, string beans, broccoli, turnips, onions, spinach, cauliflower, chestnuts, cucumbers, zucchini, carrots, mushrooms, tiny peas, cabbage, asparagus, and pimentos. The vegetables also figure prominently in the one course common to most meals, the antipasto, the richly variegated Italian hors d'oeuvre.

Italians eat a great deal of fish, what with its availability from the waters surrounding the country on three sides. Next to pasta, fish is Italy's most important category of food. Octopus, squid, and cuttlefish (*polipi, seppie,* and *calamari*) are eaten by the million. Their red mullet, sole, trout, anchovies, sea bass, sardines, lobster, oysters and clams, mackerel, eel, mussels, shrimp, crayfish, and the famous *scampi* are a revelation.

And so, you are now prepared for the foods of Italy. Whether cooked at home or eaten abroad, the Italian dishes which follow should provide great pleasure. Indeed *ne siamo certissimi:* we are quite certain of it.

❦

In using this book, the reader will find it helpful to keep the following points in mind:
• Before preparing any dish, first read every step of the recipe and be sure you understand it. The recipe is your guide—always follow its directions step by step.
• Consider the amount of cooking time you have available when selecting recipes. Some meals take longer to prepare than others; and although the end result may justify the time required, your schedule for a particular day may well dictate which meal you can cook.
• Check your cooking equipment. Before embarking on a recipe read it thoroughly and be sure you have the proper utensils on hand and within easy reach. Do not try to make do with improper equipment.
• Naturally, you'll want to have *all* the ingredients called for. To make your cooking procedure as simple and enjoyable as possible, it is best to neatly lay out all the ingredients beforehand.

Lombardy

From the Alps south to the River Po stretches Lombardy, Caesar's Cisalpine Gaul. Successive occupations by Romans, Huns and Goths, Hungarians, and (for 200 years) Spaniards have given the region's cuisine a distinctly cosmopolitan appeal. Lombardy contains the "honeymoon lakes" —Como, Garda, Lugano, and Maggiore—as well as Milan, Italy's second city and commercial center.

Butter is used extravagantly in Milanese cooking, and *polenta*, the Italian cornmeal pudding, is nearly as popular here as it is in Venice. Rice is extensively used throughout the region, cooked in stock in Pavia and Mantua, but normally eaten in Milan in the form of a saffron-rich *risotto*.

Lombardy produces excellent veal, which is used in three classic Milanese dishes: *osso buco alla milanese* (braised veal shanks served with *risotto*), *costolette di vitello alla milanese* (breaded veal cutlet), and *busecca*, the stew of veal tripe and beans that is also a specialty of Piedmont.

The Milanese make nourishing broths and also claim to make the best *minestrone* in Italy, and he would be a bold man who denied their assertion. Two dishes no visitor to Milan should miss are *cazzoeula*, a stew of pork and cabbage, and *risotto alla milanese*, in which the basic rice is enriched with bone marrow and white wine.

The cooking of Milan is faintly reminiscent of that of Germany, without the heaviness, and is also influenced by many fine French touches. In fact, the French influence can most specifically be found in the Milanese gastronomic vocabulary, much of which is more similar to French than to Italian. In the nineteenth century, French food was served exclusively in the finer Milanese restaurants and many of the wealthy Milanese sent their cooks to Paris to learn the subtle refinements of French cooking. And of course, these touches are still found in the recipes which have been passed down through Milanese families until today.

But other towns of Lombardy also have their own notable recipes. *Faraona alla valcuviana* (guinea fowl baked in clay) and *zuppa alla pavese*, hot broth poured over toast and poached eggs, are specialties of Varese and Pavia, respectively. Cremona boasts its *marubini* (ravioli stuffed with bone marrow and cheese), its *torrone* (nougat), and its unique *mostarda*, which is candied fruit in mustard syrup—the effect is reminiscent of mango chutney—and which makes a piquant accompaniment to boiled meats. And we could go on and extol the virtues of the region's stuffed turkey, salami, whipped cream, fruit pickles, sweets, candies, and its famous *panettone*, an egg cake with raisins and candied fruit peel, usually eaten with breakfast coffee and especially popular around Christmas. Comes Easter, and the Italians turn their attention to *colomba*, made of a similar dough with the addition of toasted almonds.

Desserts and pastry are extremely popular in Lombardy and many have picturesque names like "The Prince's Sweet," a plum cake soaked in different kinds of liqueur filled with an incredibly rich mixture of cheese, cream, and eggs, drenched in rum, and served well chilled. There is also "Nun's Chatter," made of egg dough, sweetened with Marsala, shaped into ribbons, fried in deep oil, and dusted with sugar.

The region produces an immense variety of cheese, of which gorgonzola and bel paese are the best known. Prodigious amounts of *crespone (salame di Milano)*, a pork and beef garlic sausage, are manufactured. What cannot be eaten locally is exported, and it is probably the most popular Italian sausage abroad.

Lombardy has no great wines but a number of adequate ones that range from the very pleasing to the rather rough. In the latter category are two very dry red wines: Sassella and Inferno. Chiaretto, a sharp, almond-tasting rosé from around Lake Garda, has great charm and is growing in popularity. Some very palatable white wines are produced from Verdicchio grapes, and they are usually called by that name. Bitter Campari, the popular apéritif, is made in the region.

The Pinot Noir and Pinot Blanc grapes are used to make Frecciarossa, a full-bodied white wine that is exported. Vermentino is a dry white wine, perfect with fish and other seafood. From Lake Garda—one of the "honeymoon lakes" mentioned above—comes Lugana, a dry white wine produced from the Trebbiano grape. Travelers to the area drink it with fish freshly caught from the lake. Cinque Terre is a wine that comes in two forms: usually quite sweet, but sometimes dry. The wines of Sassella, Grumello, Inferno, and Valgella, small villages near the Swiss border, are drunk after maturing for about four years; they are called by the names of the villages from which they come.

Milanese Vegetable Soup

MINESTRONE ALLA MILANESE

Serves 6

¼ cup pinto beans
¼ lb. Canadian bacon in 1 piece
1 leek
½ cup butter
½ small onion, peeled and chopped
bouquet garni
3 medium tomatoes, peeled
1 medium potato, peeled and diced
1 large carrot, scraped and diced
1 medium eggplant, peeled and
 diced
¾ lb. fresh peas, shelled, or 1 cup
 frozen peas
1 small celery heart, trimmed and
 sliced
9 cups chicken stock
1 cup plain uncooked rice
1 clove garlic, peeled and chopped
1 cup freshly grated parmesan
 cheese

Minestroni are a special class of Italian soups. Heavily laden with vegetables, they are eaten rather than drunk, and are often a meal in themselves. The initial sautéing of the vegetables gives the soup its characteristic flavor.

Soak the beans in cold water for 24 hours. Drain well and cook in lightly salted boiling water for about 1 hour, or until tender. Drain before using. Blanch the bacon in simmering water for 15 to 20 minutes. Drain well and cut into ¼-inch cubes.

Remove and discard the green part of the leek and trim away the root. Rinse the white part very thoroughly under cold running water and chop coarsely. Heat one third of the butter in a skillet over moderate heat and add the bacon, onion, leek, and the bouquet garni (few sprigs parsley, 1 sprig rosemary, ½ bay leaf, tied together). Cook together over moderate heat for 3 to 4 minutes, remove the herbs, add the tomatoes, and season with salt and pepper to taste. Simmer gently.

Heat the remaining butter in a second saucepan over high heat and sauté the beans, potato, carrot, eggplant, peas, and celery over moderate heat for 5 to 8 minutes. Add to the tomato mixture, simmer together for 2 to 3 minutes, then pour in the stock. Simmer over moderate heat until the vegetables are tender. Increase the heat and, when the stock boils, add the rice and simmer until *al dente*. A few moments before removing the soup from the heat, add the garlic. Serve with the cheese.

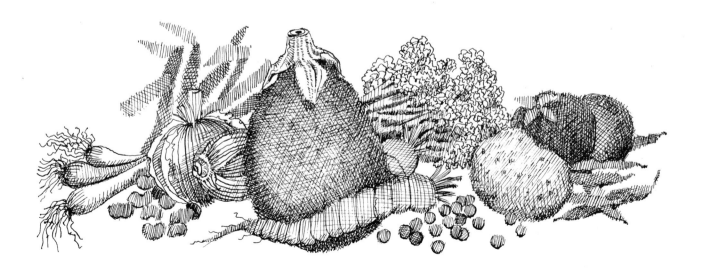

Beef-stuffed Pasta with Herb Butter

CASONSEI

Serves 6

FOR THE PASTA:
5 eggs
1 tb. melted butter
4 cups all-purpose flour
1 tsp. salt

FOR THE FILLING:
2 tbs. butter
2 cloves garlic, peeled and
    chopped
1 tb. minced parsley
½ lb. ground beef
3 tbs. fine fresh bread crumbs
1 tb. freshly grated parmesan
    cheese
pinch of nutmeg
1–2 eggs, beaten

FOR SERVING:
¾ cup butter
chopped fresh sage leaves
1 cup freshly grated parmesan
    cheese

In Lombardy, these stuffed pasta squares are traditionally served with herb butter made with sage and grated parmesan cheese. Some very old recipes gave a stuffing of pears, almonds, and chopped mixed candied peel.

To make the pasta, lightly beat the eggs and butter in a small bowl. Sift the flour and salt onto a marble slab or into a mixing bowl and make a well in the center. Pour in the egg mixture, mix to a firm dough, and knead well. Wrap in a damp cloth and set aside for about 30 minutes.

To make the filling, heat the butter in a skillet over moderate heat. Add the garlic and parsley and sauté until they begin to brown; then add the beef and sauté for about 10 minutes, stirring frequently. Remove the skillet from the heat, add the bread crumbs and cheese, and set aside in a bowl to cool. Season with the nutmeg and salt and pepper to taste and blend to a paste with the eggs.

Roll out the dough into sheets, about $\frac{1}{16}$ inch thick, on a lightly floured surface. Cut 3½-inch squares of dough and put 1 tablespoon of the filling on half of each square. Brush the edges of the square with water. Fold the uncovered half of the square over the filling and press the edges together to completely enclose the filling. Place on a lightly floured tray until required. Place a few *casonsei* at a time in a large saucepan half filled with lightly salted boiling water. Cook for about 5 minutes, removing them with a slotted spoon as they come to the surface. Drain well and place on a heated serving dish.

To serve the *casonsei*, heat the butter until golden brown, sprinkle in chopped sage leaves to taste, and pour over the pasta. Sprinkle with the cheese and serve immediately.

Lombardy

Veal foreshanks with marrow, or, as the Milanese call them, "hollow bones," are a speciality of Lombardy, Italy's major cattle-producing region. Osso buco is usually served with risotto alla milanese.

Wipe the pieces of veal with a damp cloth or paper towels and coat with flour. Melt 6 tablespoons of butter in a large skillet over high heat, add the pieces of veal, and sauté until browned. Add the onion, 1 clove of garlic, carrot, celery, marjoram, and lemon rind, and season with salt and pepper. When the mixture is lightly browned, add the wine and simmer until reduced to 1 tablespoon. Add the tomatoes and the stock. Lower the heat, cover the pan tightly, and simmer for 1 hour or more, adding a little additional stock, if necessary, to prevent the sauce from sticking.

Add the remaining clove of garlic, the grated lemon rind, and the remaining butter to the veal. Stir and simmer for 2 to 3 minutes over moderate heat. Arrange the veal in a crown shape on a round heated serving dish and cover with the sauce.

Braised Veal Shanks

OSSO BUCO ALLA MILANESE

Serves 6

2 veal foreshanks, cut into 6 pieces
all-purpose flour for coating
½ cup butter
1 small onion, peeled and chopped
    (about ½ cup)
2 cloves garlic, peeled and
    chopped
1 medium carrot, scraped and
    chopped
1 celery stalk, chopped
few sprigs marjoram, chopped
small strip thinly peeled lemon
    rind, chopped
⅔ cup dry white wine
2 ripe tomatoes, peeled and
    chopped
3–4 tbs. vegetable stock
grated rind of ½ lemon

Mixed Boiled Meats with Green Sauce

BOLLITI MISTI

Serves 8

½ lb. _cotechino_ sausage
1 lb. Canadian bacon in 1 piece
1 4-lb. capon
2 lbs. lamb rib chops
1 veal foreshank
½ lb. Italian pork sausage
1 small carrot, scraped
2 celery stalks
1 onion stuck with 2 cloves

FOR THE GREEN SAUCE:
1 large bunch parsley
2–3 anchovy fillets
3–4 pickled onions
1 small cold cooked potato
1 clove garlic, peeled and chopped
1 tb. chopped onion
6 tbs. olive oil
1 tb. vinegar

Buckwheat Pudding

POLENTA TARAGNA

Serves 6

4¼ cups water
1 tsp. salt
2 cups butter
3 cups buckwheat flour
1 lb. thinly sliced mozzarella
    cheese

Green sauce and mostarda, _a Lombardy relish, are traditional accompaniments to this and many other meat dishes._

Prick the _cotechino_ and place in a very large saucepan with the bacon. Add just enough water to cover and bring to a boil over moderate heat. Lower the heat and simmer the meats for about 1 hour. Add the capon, lamb, veal, and sausage, and enough water to cover them completely. Bring to a boil and skim the surface of the liquid. Add carrots, celery, and onion to the saucepan with a pinch of salt. Cover the saucepan and simmer for 1½ to 2 hours. Remove the different meats when they are tender, drain them, and keep them hot.

While the meats are cooking, prepare the green sauce. Place the parsley leaves in a mortar or mixing bowl with the anchovy fillets, pickled onions, potato, garlic, onion, and a pinch of salt. Pound the ingredients with a pestle or wooden rolling pin to form a soft paste. Place the mixture in a bowl and gradually add the oil, drop by drop, beating well after each addition until it resembles thick mayonnaise. Stir in the vinegar.

Serve the cooked meats as hot as possible on a wooden meat platter, with green sauce, pickles, grated fresh horseradish root, a variety of seasoned green vegetables, and boiled potatoes.

Mozzarella cheese, originally made with buffaloes' milk, was produced in accordance with a method known as pasta filata. _As buffaloes are becoming rare and the demand for the cheese is increasing, it is now commercially produced from cows' milk._

Place the water, salt, and 1 cup of butter in a saucepan over moderate heat and bring to a boil. Gradually sprinkle in the flour and, using a wooden spoon, stir constantly for about 15 minutes, adding a little additional boiling water, if necessary, to prevent the mixture from sticking. Remove the saucepan from the heat and add the remaining butter and the slices of cheese. Return the saucepan to the heat and cook gently for 30 minutes, stirring frequently. Pour into soup plates and serve immediately.

Turkey with Chestnut Stuffing

TACCHINA RIPIENA

Serves 6

1 7–9 lb. oven-ready turkey
1 lb. chestnuts
½ lb. prunes
¼ lb. Canadian bacon
1 medium cooking apple
2 medium pears
1 small white truffle (optional)
½ lb. sausage meat
¼ cup brandy
thin slices fat bacon
2 tbs. melted butter
1 cup vegetable stock
3 tbs. lemon juice
1 tb. butter

Any fowl which is low in fat content can profit by barding—placing of fat bacon over the bird. Slip a slice of bacon on either side between the leg and breast and other slices over the breast. When trussing make sure the bacon is secure on the turkey. This technique helps to keep the fowl moist. Barding differs from larding in that the latter requires insertion of fat into the meat.

In this recipe the turkey is boned and then stuffed, although some Lombard cooks prefer to leave the turkey whole and stuff the cavity with the mixture.

Wipe the turkey with a damp cloth or paper towels. Remove and discard the head and about half the neck. Break off the wings and the legs at the first joints. Using a very sharp knife, open the turkey along the backbone from the neck to the tail. Draw the turkey and discard the entrails, lungs, and kidneys. Reserve the giblets for another dish. Ease out the bones from inside the wings, little by little. Working still from the inside, remove the bones from the legs. Continue to ease out the bones until the whole carcass has been extracted. Rinse the flesh under cold running water and dry with paper towels.

Preheat the oven to 400.

Slit the chestnuts with a sharp knife and roast in the preheated oven for 10 to 15 minutes. Remove the chestnuts from the oven and, when cool enough to handle, remove and discard the outer shell and inner skin and coarsely chop the nuts. Soak the prunes; then pit and chop them. Blanch the bacon for 5 minutes in simmering water, drain, and cut into fine strips. Peel, core, and slice the apple and pears. Slice the truffle, if used.

Place the chestnuts, prunes, bacon, apple, pears, and truffle in a large mixing bowl with the sausage meat. Season with salt and pepper and the brandy and mix thoroughly. Stuff the turkey with the filling and sew up securely along the backbone. Sprinkle with salt and pepper and cover the breast with the slices of fat bacon. Truss the turkey into its original shape with fine white string. Place the turkey in a buttered roasting pan and roast in the preheated oven for 20 minutes. Lower the heat to 325 and roast for an additional 2 hours. About 20 minutes before the end of the cooking time, remove the turkey from the oven and discard the slices of fat. Brush the turkey with the melted butter and return to the oven.

Remove the turkey from the roasting pan and place on a heated serving dish. Remove and discard the string. Let the turkey stand at room temperature for 15 to 20 minutes to make it easier to carve. Meanwhile, mix the stock into the juices left in the pan and simmer for 2 to 3 minutes, stirring with a wooden spoon to prevent the gravy from sticking. Strain through a fine sieve, skim off the fat, and stir in the lemon juice and butter. Serve the gravy separately.

Traditionally, polenta *is cooked in an unlined copper cauldron with a rounded bottom, a* paiolo. *If no* paiolo *is available, a large, heavy saucepan can be substituted.*

Bring the water and salt to a boil in a large, heavy saucepan. Sprinkle in one third of the cornmeal, a little at a time. Using a wooden spoon, stir the mixture constantly. As the mixture thickens, add the 3 to 4 tablespoons boiling water. After 15 minutes, sprinkle in another third of the cornmeal, stirring constantly. Gradually add the remaining cornmeal and continue stirring until the mixture is well blended. The *polenta* is perfectly cooked when it comes away easily from the side of the pan. This takes 30 to 45 minutes. To make the cornmeal easier to digest, and to remove its slightly bitter taste, it is advisable to extend the cooking period to at least 1 hour, stirring frequently.

The *polenta* may be eaten very hot with various sauces and garnishes, or cold, sliced in the classic way using strong, fine thread rather than a knife, and served with butter and freshly grated parmesan cheese. It may also be cut into thick slices and fried. Sliced cold *polenta* is a good substitute for bread, especially with a beef stew.

Cornmeal Pudding

POLENTA

Makes 2 cups

4¼ cups water
1 tsp. salt
2 cups yellow cornmeal
3–4 tbs. boiling water

> *Polenta* is not a sophisticated dish; it corresponds to cornmeal mush. There are, however, degrees of refinement, depending on whether the cornmeal is coarsely or finely ground, or whether it is removed from the fire while still relatively liquid or allowed to thicken, and, finally, on the intuition of the cook.

In days gone by the servants rose at dawn to beat the chops rhythmically on wood, first one side, then the other. It was thought that this treatment would make the meat tender.

Remove and discard any skin and excess fat from the chops. Flatten the veal lightly with a meat mallet or a rolling pin. Lightly beat the eggs. Season the veal with pepper and coat with flour, then dip in the beaten egg and coat with the bread crumbs. Heat the butter in a skillet over moderate heat and sauté the veal for 10 to 15 minutes, or until lightly browned on each side. Arrange the chops on a heated serving plate and pour the butter in which they were cooked over them. Sprinkle with salt. Garnish with the lemons and serve immediately. A dash of nutmeg may be sprinkled over the chops.

Milanese Veal Chops

COSTOLETTE DI VITELLO ALLA MILANESE

Serves 6

6 veal rib chops
2 eggs
all-purpose flour for coating
1½ cups toasted bread crumbs
½ cup butter
3 lemons, halved
pinch of nutmeg (optional)

Savoy Cabbage and Rice Soup

MINESTRA DI RISO E VERZA

Serves 6

1 small Savoy cabbage
¼ cup butter
½ cup ground ham fat
1 small onion, peeled and chopped
9 cups chicken stock or water
1 cup plain uncooked rice
1 tb. minced chopped parsley
1 cup freshly grated parmesan
    cheese

Ideally served in the depth of winter, this warming soup is also served on the feast of St. Anthony.

Remove and discard the coarse outer leaves from the cabbage. Remove and discard the center core and tough stems. Rinse the leaves under cold running water and drain well. Simmer the cabbage in very little lightly salted boiling water for 5 to 6 minutes. Drain well and chop coarsely. Heat 1 tablespoon of butter in a large skillet over low heat. Sauté the cabbage in the butter and then cover with boiling water. Raise the heat to high and bring to a boil. Cook for 5 to 10 minutes, or until tender, and remove from the heat.

Heat the remaining butter in a saucepan with the ham fat, add the onion, and sauté until lightly browned. Add the cabbage and the cooking liquid. Mix well and season with salt and pepper to taste. Add the stock and bring to a boil. Add the rice and cook for 15 to 20 minutes, or until tender. A few seconds before removing the pan from the heat, add the parsley. Serve immediately with the cheese.

> All cabbage types, if fresh, are a high and inexpensive source of vitamin C. Savoy cabbages are a loose-leaved variety that are popular for their elegant texture. If Savoy cabbage is unavailable, substitute any firm-headed green cabbage in this soup.

Tripe in Meat Sauce

TRIPPA ALLA MILANESE

Serves 6

2 lbs. precooked tripe
2 tsps. salt
1¼ cups meat sauce (see page 64)
1 cup freshly grated parmesan
    cheese

The origin of parmesan cheese, used so extensively in Italian cuisine, is not really known. It is unique in that it does not form elasticlike threads as it melts, and it will keep for years, the longer the better!

Cut the tripe into strips, about 4 inches long and ¾ inch wide. Place in a saucepan, barely cover with water, and add the salt. Bring to a boil over moderate heat. Cover tightly and simmer for about 1¼ hours.

About 15 minutes before the end of the cooking time, drain the tripe and return to the saucepan with the meat sauce. Adjust the seasoning, if necessary, and finish cooking over moderate heat. Pour the tripe into a deep heated serving dish and serve with the cheese.

Many Milanese dishes, including this risotto, *are colored with saffron. There was a fourteenth-century belief that gold was a panacea for all ills, so food was often gilded before it was served. On poorer tables saffron was used instead of gold.*

Heat about 5 tablespoons of the butter in a saucepan over low heat and add the onion, bone marrow, and pepper. Sauté the onion until soft, but not brown, then add the wine and reduce it by half. Add the rice and a pinch of salt and cook for 2 to 3 minutes, stirring constantly. Add the saffron powder and stock and bring to a boil, still stirring. Simmer for about 15 minutes, stirring constantly and adding a little additional hot stock, if necessary, to prevent the rice from sticking to the saucepan.

Remove the saucepan from the heat when the rice is *al dente*. Add the remaining butter and 3 to 4 tablespoons of the cheese. Set aside for 2 to 3 minutes in a warm place; then transfer to a heated serving dish. Serve immediately with the remaining cheese.

Milanese Rice

RISOTTO ALLA MILANESE

Serves 6

1 cup butter
¼ onion, peeled and finely
    chopped
3 tbs. bone marrow
⅔ cup dry white wine
2¼ cups plain uncooked rice
pinch of saffron powder
about 4¼ cups vegetable stock
1 cup freshly grated parmesan
    cheese

Marrow-stuffed Pasta

MARUBINI

Serves 6

FOR THE PASTA:
5 eggs
4 cups all-purpose flour
1 tsp. salt
1 tb. olive oil

FOR THE FILLING:
5 cups dry bread crumbs
1½ cups freshly grated parmesan
    cheese
½ cup melted bone marrow
pinch of nutmeg
2 egg yolks
2–3 tbs. beef stock
1 egg, beaten

FOR SERVING:
¾ cup melted butter
1 cup grated parmesan cheese

Marrow is found in the long shank bones. The bigger the animal, the more marrow the bones contain. It is extremely nutritious and very tasty.

Lightly beat the eggs and olive oil together in a small bowl. Sift the flour and salt onto a marble slab or into a mixing bowl and make a well in the center. Pour in the eggs and oil, mix to a firm smooth dough, and knead well. Wrap in a damp cloth and set aside for about 30 minutes.

To make the filling, mix together the bread crumbs, cheese, bone marrow, nutmeg, salt, and pepper. Add the egg yolks and mix to a soft dough, adding the stock if necessary. Roll the dough into two thin sheets, about ¹⁄₁₆ inch thick. Brush the surface of the first sheet of pasta with beaten egg and, using a pastry bag and ½-inch tip, pipe small amounts of filling onto the sheet about 2 inches apart. Cover with the second sheet of pasta, brush with the egg, and seal the layers together by pressing the spaces between the filling with the fingertips.

Cut into squares, using a pastry wheel or a sharp knife, and place on a lightly floured board. Cook the *marubini*, a few at a time, in a large saucepan half filled with lightly salted boiling water, for 8 to 10 minutes, or until they rise to the surface. Remove with a perforated spoon and drain well.

To serve, heat the butter in a saucepan over moderate heat until it is lightly browned. Arrange the *marubini* in layers in a heated serving dish alternated with the butter and half the cheese. Serve immediately with the remaining cheese.

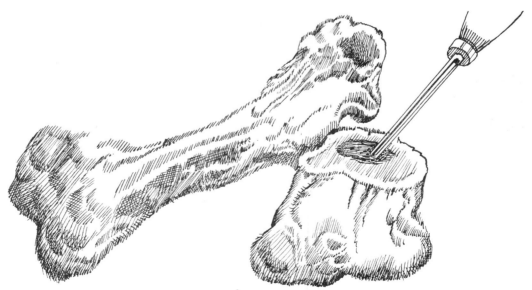

marrow bone

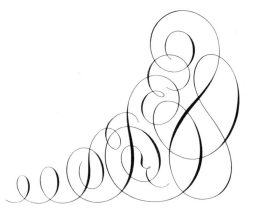

Liguria

Liguria, the smallest province in Italy, runs eastward from the French border in a long narrow strip along the Mediterranean coast. Its chief city is Genoa, which has been a flourishing seaport for more than a thousand years and which monopolized, with Venice, the ferrying of spices between Asia and Europe. However, unlike Venice, the Genoese did not retain many of these spices for their cooking. Instead they preferred their locally grown herbs, and still do today.

The cooking of the region also makes abundant use of local olive oil, which is claimed to be one of the best in Italy. However, in recent years so little of it has been produced that much of the oil used in Ligurian cooking is now imported. The reason for this decrease in olive oil production is that much of the land formerly used for olive groves is now being turned into commercial flower fields. And, as a natural result of the cultivation of flower fields, Liguria has become an important exporter of honey.

Basil is perhaps the most famous Genoese herb since it forms the basis of the famed *pesto* sauce (made from basil, garlic, cheese, and olive oil). It is said in Genoa that only locally grown basil imparts the authentic tang. *Pesto* is frequently served with soup, fish, and meat and is one of the best sauces for pasta. Other delightful Genoese herbs include sage, rosemary, marjoram, and *scorzonera*.

Herbs, excellent produce from the rich farms, and the enormous variety of fish from the Mediterranean Sea form the backbone of the Ligurian cuisine, which has much in common with the cuisine of nearby southern France: a fish stew, *ciuppin*, flavored with garlic, onions, and herbs, is similar to *bouillabaisse; burrida* is a more elaborate version that may contain up to a dozen different fish and shellfish, sometimes with octopus and squid for good measure. And a specialty of San Remo that closely resembles the *pissaladière* of the French Riviera is *sardenaria*, a pizza made with salted sardines, tomatoes, garlic, and fresh oregano.

Two fried dishes from this region that are worthy of mention are *fricassea di pollo*, which consists of pieces of chicken fried with onion and served with a sauce of egg, lemon, and parsley, and *frito allo stecco*, which is a combination of veal, sweetbreads, brains, and mushrooms that is dipped in egg and breadcrumbs before frying. A baked dish, *riso arrosto alla genovese*, is a casserole of rice, sausage, peas, artichokes, mushrooms, cheese, and onions. *Trenette al pesto* and *gnocchi al pesto* are two specialties served with the ubiquitous *pesto* sauce. *Trenette* are very thin noodles, and *gnocchi* are boiled dumplings made from potato dough. *Cappon magro* is a rather unique dish of pickled fish and boiled vegetables, and *zuppa di datteri* is a very flavorful seafood soup.

A fascinating Genoese dish is *sbira*, which stands in much the same relationship to humble tripe and onions as does caviar to kipper paste. The Genoese cook uses two kinds of tripe, "blanket" and "honeycomb," a great variety of herbs and vegetables, and an extremely rich beef stock. Another Genoese specialty, sweetbreads and liver coated with egg and bread crumbs, then fried, is called *bianco e nero* (black and white). Ravioli is perhaps the most popular of all local dishes and is prepared in many ways with a variety of fillings. Characteristically, Ligurian dishes have long and complex lists of ingredients. For example, turkey is boiled in a soup that contains onion, celery, parsley, carrots, bay leaves, sage, rosemary, thyme, cloves, nutmeg, and truffles. *Cima di vitello ripiena* is a relatively simple regional dish, consisting merely of a breast of veal stuffed with brains, sweetbreads, artichoke hearts, eggs, peas, and rosemary. A pastry shell is sometimes substituted for the breast of veal. As regards desserts, Genoa has a whole range of *budini* (puddings), and its own variety of *pandolce*, a light *brioche* with raisins and candied peel. The town of La Spezia is noted for its macaroons (*amaretti*).

Genoese cuisine seems to peak when an all-out effort is made to celebrate one of the many religious holidays. At Easter the *torta Pasqualina*, a richer than usual double-crusted tart, is served. Made with meat stuffing for holidays and meatless on fast days, it is served slightly cooled from the oven, and is also excellent when served cold.

The wines of the region are neither outstanding in quality nor numerous. Perhaps the best come from the Cinque Terre region near La Spezia. Schicchetrà is a rather sweet and heavy dessert wine. The other noteworthy wines are also white, but without exception extremely dry. Names to look for are Coronata, Polcevera, and Vermentino Ligure. A good *grappa* is distilled from grape pressings in the town of Chiavari.

Noodles with Pesto

TAGLIATELLE CON PESTO

Serves 6

5 eggs
1 tb. olive oil
4 cups all-purpose flour
1 tsp. salt
3 medium potatoes, peeled and thickly sliced (about 3 cups)
½ cup freshly grated pecorino sardo cheese
pesto (see below)

Basil, Garlic, and Cheese Sauce

PESTO

Serves 6

1 large bunch fresh basil
few spinach leaves (optional)
few sprigs parsley (optional)
few sprigs marjoram (optional)
3 cloves garlic, peeled
pinch coarse (kosher) salt
¾–1 cup freshly grated pecorino cheese
6 tbs. olive oil
2–3 tbs. liquid

Tagliatelle made its first appearance at a dinner in honor of Lucrezia Borgia. The cook was inspired by her long blonde hair and devised these light ribbonlike noodles. You can substitute egg noodles for the homemade tagliatelle.

Lightly beat together the eggs and olive oil in a small bowl. Sift the flour and salt onto a marble pastry slab or into a mixing bowl and make a well in the center. Pour in the eggs and the oil, mix to a firm, smooth dough, and knead well. Wrap in a damp cloth and set aside for about 30 minutes.

Roll the dough into sheets, about ¹⁄₁₆ inch thick. Fold each sheet in half lengthwise, then fold in half lengthwise again, several times. With a sharp knife, cut the dough into noodles 1 inch wide. Unfold the noodles and place on a floured surface. Cover with a lightly floured cloth and set aside for 10 to 15 minutes.

Simmer the potatoes in lightly salted boiling water until they are almost cooked. Add the noodles and continue simmering until they are *al dente*. Drain the noodles and potatoes and reserve 3 tablespoons of the liquid. Place them on an oval heated serving dish, sprinkle immediately with the cheese and the reserved cooking liquid, and mix lightly. Pour the *pesto* over the mixture and bring to the table. Mix together until the potatoes and noodles are well coated and serve immediately.

❧

Although pesto *in its original and traditional form is made with basil as the only herb, it may be made using spinach, marjoram, and parsley, as in this recipe.*

Remove the stems from the basil, wash it well, and dry completely in a towel. Clean the spinach, parsley, and marjoram, if used, in a similar manner. Put a bit of the basil in a mortar or large bowl and pound it with a pestle. Gradually add the remaining basil, spinach, parsley, marjoram, garlic, and salt and continue to pound carefully, stirring occasionally, until the mixture is reduced to a smooth pulp. Add the cheese and pound to a well-blended paste.

Add the oil drop by drop, beating constantly, as if making a mayonnaise. Blend the liquid into the paste until smooth. Preferably use water in which pasta has been cooked. Alternatively, cold water may be used.

Stuffed Pasta with Walnut Sauce

PANSÔTI CON SALSA
DI NOCI

Serves 6

FOR THE FILLING:
2 oz. lamb brains
2 oz. lamb sweetbreads
¾ lb. spinach
½ lb. beet leaves
½ lb. fresh borage or additional
  beet and spinach leaves
½ lb. watercress
5 tbs. butter
1 cup ricotta cheese
2 eggs
1 clove garlic
pinch of nutmeg

FOR THE PASTA:
4 eggs
3 tbs. warm water
6 cups all-purpose flour
1 tsp. salt
1 egg, beaten

FOR THE SAUCE:
1 clove garlic
1 cup shelled walnuts
½ cup pignolia nuts
about ⅔ cup olive oil
1 cup freshly grated parmesan
  cheese

> Literally translated, *pansôti* means "pot-bellied," informing the cook that the pasta should be well-filled.

The walnut sauce is a specialty of Liguria and is often served with pansôti—*fat little squares of ravioli.*

To make the filling, soak the brains and sweetbreads in cold water for 1 hour. Blanch them in boiling water, drain well, and remove skin, blood vessels, and coarse tissue. Rinse the spinach, beet leaves, borage, and watercress under cold running water. Remove and discard any tough stems and veins, and shred all the leaves. Cook the leaves in lightly salted boiling water until tender. Drain thoroughly and press through a sieve into a large bowl. Heat the butter in a skillet over moderate heat and sauté the brains and sweetbreads for 5 to 6 minutes, stirring frequently. Press through a sieve into the bowl with the sieved greens.

Sieve the ricotta cheese, beat the eggs, peel and crush the garlic, and stir the brain mixture along with the eggs, garlic, and nutmeg; season with salt to taste. Mix to a stiff paste. With floured hands, roll the paste into small balls, about the size of a walnut, and set aside while making the pasta.

To make the pasta, lightly beat together the eggs and water in a small bowl. Sift the flour and salt onto a marble slab or into a mixing bowl and make a well in the center. Pour in the eggs and water, mix to a firm smooth dough, and knead well. Wrap the dough in a damp cloth and set aside for about 30 minutes.

Roll the dough into two sheets, about 1/16 inch thick, and brush the first sheet with beaten egg. Place the balls of filling about 2 inches apart on the first sheet of dough. Cover with the second sheet and press firmly between the rounds of filling to seal together the two layers. Using a fluted pastry wheel or a sharp knife, cut *pansôti* into 2-inch squares. Place on a floured surface.

Preheat the oven to 400.

To make the sauce, peel the garlic and grind with the walnuts and pignolas. Press the mixture through a sieve into a bowl. Add the olive oil, drop by drop, beating constantly as if making a mayonnaise, until a thick coating mixture is formed. Add more oil, if necessary. Place a few *pansôti* at a time in a large saucepan half filled with lightly salted boiling water. Simmer for about 15 minutes. Remove with a perforated spoon and drain well. Place in a heated serving dish, sprinkle with the parmesan cheese, and cover with walnut sauce. Mix well and place in the preheated oven for 3 to 4 minutes. Serve immediately.

Veal in White Wine

VITELLO ALL' UCCELLETTO

Serves 6

1 lb. veal tenderloin
¼ cup butter
1 tb. oil
2 bay leaves
6 tbs. dry white wine

In Italy, this dish is cooked in a tegame, _which is a round double-handled aluminum pan, but a skillet may be used._

Cut the veal into ¼-inch by 3-inch strips and season with salt and pepper. Heat the butter and oil in a _tegame_ or skillet over moderate heat, add the bay leaves, and lightly sauté. Raise the heat, add the veal, and sauté on each side for 3 to 4 minutes, or until golden brown. Lower the heat and cook for an additional minute.

Arrange the veal slices on a heated serving plate and keep hot. Add the wine to the skillet, reduce it almost completely, and pour over the veal. Serve immediately.

> Italian veal, or _vitello_, is the flesh of a calf that has never fed on anything but its mother's milk, and which has been slaughtered when a few weeks or months old. It is of superb quality not known in the United States; it is almost white in color and very finely textured. Its flavor is bland which is why the Italians use savory touches of herbs, ham, and wine.

Vegetable and Pasta Soup

MINESTRONE CON BATTUTO D'AGLIO E BASILICO

Serves 6

10 oz. _bavette_, or other narrow spaghetti
¼ cup olive oil
3 cloves garlic, peeled and chopped
⅓ cup ground ham fat
1 medium tomato, peeled and sliced
4¼ cups cold water
3 tbs. finely chopped basil
1 cup freshly grated pecorino cheese

Bavette _are rods of pasta, each with a central groove, like a pencil split longitudinally with the lead removed._

Break the _bavette_ into 1- to 1½-inch pieces. Heat the olive oil in a saucepan over moderate heat, add the garlic and ham fat, and sauté until lightly browned. Add the slices of tomato, stir for a few minutes, and then add the water. Season with salt and pepper. Bring the contents of the saucepan to a boil. Add the _bavette_ and cook for 10 to 12 minutes, or until _al dente_. Remove the saucepan from the heat and add the basil and 3 tablespoons of the cheese. Serve hot, passing the remaining cheese separately.

> Pecorino is a type of romano cheese made from ewe's milk. This off-white, medium-sharp grating cheese comes in many varieties. Hard and tangy, it is most often used for cooking but can be enjoyed as an eating cheese as well. The flavor of pecorino is similar to that of parmesan; however, it is much sharper and is usually less expensive.

Although lamb brains and sweetbreads can be used, those of the calf are much preferred for their finer texture and more delicate flavor.

Rub the brains with the cut side of half a lemon and soak in cold water for about 1 hour. Drain well and dry with a cloth or paper towels. Rub with lemon again, replace in cold water, and soak for an additional hour, until the brains become white. Blanch in boiling water, then drain well, and remove any skin, blood vessels, and coarse tissue. Soak the sweetbreads in cold water for 30 minutes to remove the excess blood. Place the sweetbreads in a saucepan, cover with water, add the vinegar, and simmer for 15 minutes. Slice the brains, sweetbreads, and liver and season with salt and pepper. Coat with the flour, dip them into the egg, and then coat with the bread crumbs.

Heat the olive oil in a skillet until very hot and fry the prepared meat slices in it until golden brown and crisp. Remove from the skillet and drain well on paper towels. Slice the remaining lemons into wedges. Arrange on a heated serving dish and garnish with the lemon wedges.

❧

Italy is Europe's largest producer of rice and the crop has been cultivated there since the sixteenth century.

Rinse the peas under cold running water and drain in a colander. Heat one third of the butter in a saucepan over moderate heat. Add the onion and sauté until lightly browned. Add the sausage meat and salt and pepper and mix lightly. Add the peas, mushrooms, and bread cubes and continue cooking for 5 to 10 minutes, stirring frequently. Stir in the gravy and bring the mixture to a boil. Stir in the rice and add the stock gradually as the rice absorbs the liquid. Simmer for about 15 to 20 minutes, or until the rice is *al dente*. Remove the saucepan from the heat. Blend in the remaining butter and half the cheese.

Preheat the oven to 400.

Pour the mixture into an ovenproof casserole and smooth the top with the back of a spoon. Place in the preheated oven and bake for 15 to 20 minutes, or until a golden crust forms on top. Serve immediately with the remaining cheese.

Fried Liver and Sweetbreads

BIANCO E NERO

Serves 6

¾ lb. calf or lamb brains
4 lemons
¾ lb. calf or lamb sweetbreads
1 tb. vinegar
¾ lb. lamb liver
about ¼ cup all-purpose flour
1 egg, beaten
1 cup fine dry bread crumbs
6 tbs. olive oil

Genoese Rice

RISO ARROSTO ALLA GENOVESE

Serves 6

1½ lbs. fresh peas, shelled (about 1½ cups)
½ cup butter
1 small onion, peeled and chopped (about ½ cup)
½ lb. sausage
6 dried mushrooms, soaked, drained, and chopped, or 6 fresh mushrooms, chopped
½ long Italian bread, cubed
1¼ cups roast beef gravy
2½ cups uncooked rice
about 4½ cups beef stock or water
1 cup freshly grated parmesan cheese

Easter Pie

TORTA PASQUALINA

Serves 6

FOR THE PASTRY:
8 cups all-purpose flour
1½ tsps. salt
1 tb. olive oil
2½ cups water

FOR THE FILLING:
¼ lb. young, small-veined beet
    leaves or very young artichokes
½ cup grated parmesan cheese
1½ tsps. chopped fresh marjoram
    and parsley, or 1 tsp. dried
    marjoram and parsley
¾ lb. ricotta cheese
2 tbs. all-purpose flour
¼ cup light cream
3 tbs. olive oil
6 eggs
¼ cup melted butter

A springform pan has a removable rim which detaches from the bottom to facilitate removal of the baked food. It is most useful for this type of pie, which is too delicate in texture to stand much handling. If a 14-by-12-inch pan is unavailable, separate the pie into two 8-inch springforms.

Easter dinner is probably the most elaborate meal of the year in Italy, and each family has many special recipes that are prepared for that day. This traditional cheese and greens pie takes some time to make, but the effort is rewarded by the delicious and festive result.

Sift the flour and salt onto a marble slab or into a mixing bowl and make a well in the center. Pour in the olive oil and water and mix to a very soft dough. Knead well and divide into 20 pieces. Place the pieces on a floured cloth and cover with a damp cloth.

Rinse the beet leaves under cold running water. Drain well and shred finely. Cook in lightly salted boiling water for 8 to 10 minutes. Drain the beet leaves, squeeze them to remove the excess moisture and spread on a large plate. Sprinkle with half the parmesan cheese and the marjoram and parsley. If using artichokes, discard the coarse outer leaves, clean the remaining leaves thoroughly, cut into fine strips, and cook in lightly salted boiling water. Reserve the hearts for another use. Drain well and continue as above.

Blend the ricotta cheese with the remaining flour and press through a sieve into a bowl. Add the cream and salt and pepper. Roll out 10 pieces of the dough into very thin round sheets, each about 14 inches in diameter. Place in layers in a 12-inch-deep springform pan, brushing each layer except the last with olive oil. Carefully press them firmly against the bottom and sides of the pan. Spread the beet leaves evenly over the top layer of dough. Sprinkle with olive oil and cover with the ricotta mixture. With the back of a spoon, make 6 hollows in the cheese mixture and carefully crack 1 egg into each one, without breaking the yolks. Pour a little of the melted butter over each egg. Season with salt and pepper to taste and sprinkle with the remaining parmesan cheese.

Preheat the oven to 375.

Roll out the remaining pieces of dough to the same size as the previous pieces. Place in layers over the mixture, brushing each one with oil. Trim the surplus dough overlapping the edge of the pan. Make a braid with these trimmings and place it around the edge of the pie. Brush the surface of the dough with oil and lightly prick with a fork to allow the steam to escape during cooking, without breaking the egg yolks. Place in the preheated oven and bake for 50 to 60 minutes. Easter pie is excellent eaten either hot or cold.

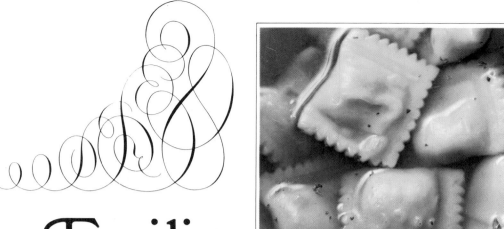

Emilia-Romagna

The twin provinces of Emilia and Romagna, whose chief city is Bologna, form the heartland of classic Italian gastronomy. Here are Parma, famous for its ham and cheese, and Bologna, renowned for its sauces. Here, it is said, the best pork in Italy is raised, and the region's sausages alone would entitle it to culinary fame: *cotechino*, one of the greatest *salame*, is a specialty of Modena; *mortadella*, the famous Bologna sausage, contains caraway seeds and white wine; *lugànega*, made throughout the region, is the basis (with tomatoes, sage, and olive oil) of *salsiccie alla romagnola*. It is from Bologna that American boloney takes its name. Boloney, however, lacks the subtlety of its forebear, *mortadella*.

The provinces contain some of the best and most fertile land in Italy, and they produce excellent wheat, sugar beets, tomatoes, asparagus, and fruits such as apples, pears, and beautiful, delicious dark cherries. Fine pasture is responsible for the superior beef and veal of the region. The inhabitants lay claim to producing the best pasta dishes in the country, and one can find little reason for disagreement. Of primary importance is the quality of their pasta dough, which emanates from their own local wheat. The wheat is ground into a type of pure wheat flour; next it is strained through a silk sieve, and then kneaded. Finally, the pasta dough is rolled to a thinness approaching translucence. One of the best known of the region's pasta dishes, all of which start from this carefully prepared dough, is *tagliatelle*. According to Bolognese legend, *tagliatelle* was inspired by the flaxen hair of Lucrezia Borgia.

Among the regional specialties are *brodetto* and *zampone*. *Brodetto* is a fish soup of great variety and richness, and *zampone* is the skin of a pig's foot, stuffed with seasoned pork, and boiled for four hours. It is eaten in thin slices with mustard. *Anolini* are a form of ravioli with a beef and bacon stuffing, poached in broth and served with butter and cheese. In *pasticcio di anolini* the *anolini* are encased in sweet pastry and baked in the oven, producing a bizarre but agreeable combination of flavors. *Tortellini* are small round pieces of dough stuffed with such things as sausage, pork, prosciutto, and cheese, served either in consommé or alone, in which case they are smothered in a variety of sauces. According to many, *tortellini* is the greatest gastronomic speciality of Bologna. Bolognese can become passionate about this dish. A Bolognese poet once wrote: "If the first father of the human race was lost for an apple, what would he not have done for a plate of *tortellini*?" A nineteenth-century writer proclaimed: "*Tortellini* is more essential than the sun for Sunday, or love for a woman."

Lasagne, prepared in a number of ways, is said to be a creation of the region. When correctly made, Bolognese sauce (or *ragù*, as the inhabitants of Bologna call it) is the best of all accompaniments to pasta, although it was originally designed specifically to be eaten with *lasagne verde*. This region is also famous for *prosciutto*, a ham which is often served raw with fruit like melon or figs, but is sometimes tossed in butter and eaten with spaghetti. Then there is the very expensive, highly prized *culatello di zibello*, cured pork butt steeped in white wine, and the delicious *fritto misto*, a "mixed fry" containing such ingredients as small pieces of calf liver, brains, chicken croquettes, skewered meats, zucchini, deep-fried cauliflower, and artichokes.

The provinces are the home of parmesan cheese, the most popular of all Italian cheeses. It is used as a basic ingredient in many of the region's dishes: for example, in *petti di pollo alla bolognese*, fried breasts of chicken, topped with ham, grated parmesan cheese, and melted butter, or *costolette bolognese*, where veal replaces the chicken.

Filetti di tacchino consists of turkey and ham, sliced and baked with cheese, white wine, and thinly sliced truffles. *Involtini* is a veal dish, in which veal is rolled and then stuffed with ham, sage, and parmesan cheese before being stewed. Clams are served with rice and a parsley and tomato sauce in a specialty called *risotto alle vongole*. The ubiquitous *prosciutto* turns up in *cotoletta al prosciutto* accompanying breaded fried veal cutlets. *Cappelletti* is pasta dough shaped like little hats and then filled with cheese, meat, and spices.

The region's bakers maintain a high standard. The bread is as good as anywhere in Europe. And there is the widest possible range of little cakes and *gâteaux*, for which the town of Parma is particularly noted.

The wines of Emilia and Romagna fall short of excellence, but cannot be bettered as honest table wines. Notable among the red wines is Lambrusco, an unusual sparkling wine that can be obtained either sweet or dry. Sangiovese, from Forlì in Emilia, is full-bodied and virile, as is the very dark red Scorza Amara from Parma. Two dry white wines suitable for drinking with fish are Vino del Bosco and Malvasia di Maiatico, while Albana is a dessert wine of some charm.

Bolognese Sauce

SALSA BOLOGNESE

Makes 2 cups

2 tbs. butter
½ small onion, peeled and chopped
½ small carrot, chopped
1 clove garlic, peeled and chopped
1 celery stalk, chopped
3 tbs. olive oil
¼ cup ham, chopped
3 dried mushrooms, soaked and
    drained, or 3 fresh mushrooms,
    chopped
½ lb. beef, coarsely ground or
    minced (1 cup)
6 tbs. dry red wine
1 tb. minced parsley
1 tb. minced marjoram
2 tsps. all-purpose flour
2 large tomatoes, peeled and
    chopped

This is probably the best-known Italian sauce. If it is well-made with the very best ingredients, it is a perfect accompaniment to pasta dishes. It will keep under refrigeration for several days.

Heat the butter in a skillet over moderate heat. Add the onion, carrot, garlic, and celery and sauté until lightly browned. Remove the skillet from the heat and set aside.

Heat the olive oil in a large skillet over moderate heat. Add the ham or bacon and sauté until lightly browned. Add the sautéed vegetables, mushrooms, and beef. Cook for 10 to 15 minutes over moderate heat, stirring occasionally. Then pour in the wine, add the parsley and marjoram, and season with salt and pepper.

When the wine is reduced to less than a tablespoon, remove the skillet from the heat and stir in the flour. Mix thoroughly, return the skillet to the heat, and cook the mixture very gently for 10 to 15 minutes, stirring constantly. Add the tomatoes to the sauce. To prevent the sauce from sticking, add 1 tablespoon of water occasionally. Remove the saucepan from the heat as soon as the sauce is well blended and slightly thickened. Use as required.

Throughout Italy, large juicy tomatoes are one of the most plentiful commodities. This sauce can be made in double or triple quantities and frozen. It is excellent as a base for meat sauces and can also be used alone on spaghetti or pizza. If fresh marjoram is available, it will make an appreciable difference in the flavor.

Heat the lard and ham fat in a large saucepan over moderate heat, add the garlic, and sauté until lightly browned. Add the onion, carrot, celery, parsley, marjoram, clove, and paprika. Stir together until lightly browned; then pour in the wine and simmer until the wine is almost completely reduced. Add the tomatoes and season with salt. Cover the saucepan tightly and simmer over moderate heat for about 1 hour, stirring occasionally. From time to time, add 1 tablespoon of hot water to prevent the sauce from becoming too thick. Remove the saucepan from the heat and strain the sauce through a fine sieve. Use as required.

Tomato Sauce

SUGO DI POMODORO
Makes 2 to 3 cups

¼ cup lard
⅓ cup finely ground ham fat
1 clove garlic, peeled and crushed
1 medium onion, peeled and
   chopped (about ¾ cup)
1 small carrot, scraped and
   chopped
1 celery stalk, chopped
few sprigs parsley
few sprigs marjoram
1 clove
pinch of paprika
⅔ cup dry white wine
2 lbs. tomatoes, peeled and
   chopped

Cheese-stuffed Pasta in Bouillon

CAPPELLETTI IN BRODO

Serves 6

FOR THE PASTA:
4 eggs
2 tsps. olive oil
3 cups all-purpose flour
¾ tsp. salt

FOR THE FILLING:
1 cup ricotta cheese, or half ricotta
    and half cacio cheese
1¼ cups grated parmesan cheese
1 egg
1 egg yolk
¼ tsp. grated lemon rind
pinch of mixed dried herbs (sage,
    parsley, thyme, rosemary, and
    bay leaves)
11 cups beef or chicken bouillon

Cappelletti *means "little hats," and these ravioli appear throughout northern Italy with a variety of fillings. This mixed cheese stuffing is typical of Emilia-Romagna. You can substitute commercial ravioli for the homemade* cappelletti.

To make the pasta, lightly beat together the eggs and olive oil in a small bowl. Sift the flour and salt onto a marble slab or into a mixing bowl and make a well in the center. Pour in the eggs and oil. Mix to a smooth dough and knead well. Wrap in a damp cloth and set aside for about 30 minutes.

To make the filling, mix together the ricotta cheese, ¼ cup parmesan cheese, egg, egg yolk, lemon rind, and herbs. Season with salt to taste. Roll the mixture into balls about the size of small walnuts, and place on a floured surface.

Knead the dough lightly and roll out into sheets, ¹⁄₁₆ inch thick. Using a 2-inch floured cutter, cut out circles of dough. (Alternatively, cut 2-inch squares, using a floured sharp knife.) Place one ball of filling in the center of each piece of dough. Fold in half and firmly press the edges together, to form the *cappelletti*. Press the leftover dough into a ball and repeat the process until all the pasta and filling are used. Bring the bouillon to a boil. Add the *cappelletti* and simmer for 5 to 10 minutes, or until they rise to the surface. Serve immediately in heated soup dishes, with the remaining cheese passed separately.

Deep-fried Artichoke Hearts

FONDI DI CARCIOFO

Serves 4

4 large or 8 small artichokes
1 tb. lemon juice
3 tbs. all-purpose flour
oil for deep-frying

Fresh vegetables are abundant in Italy, and they are generally cooked quickly to preserve their color and texture. Here is an example of the simple and delicious manner in which Italians prepare their excellent vegetables.

Remove and discard the leaves and choke from each artichoke, leaving only the heart. Cut each heart into quarters or halves and place in a bowl. Cover with water and add the lemon juice. Set aside for 1 to 2 hours. Drain well on paper towels. Coat the hearts with the flour and deep-fry in hot oil for 2 to 3 minutes, or until golden brown. Drain well and serve hot.

Sausage-stuffed Pasta in Bouillon

ANOLINI IN BRODO

Serves 6

FOR THE FILLING:
6 tbs. butter
1 tsp. chopped carrot
1 tsp. chopped celery
1 tsp. chopped onion
1 small *cotechino* sausage, peeled
¾ lb. beef round steak
1¼ cups beef or chicken bouillon
1¼ cups toasted fine bread crumbs
3 tbs. freshly grated parmesan
  cheese
pinch of ground nutmeg
3 eggs

FOR THE PASTA:
5 eggs
1 tsp. olive oil
4 cups all-purpose flour
1 tsp. salt
1 egg, beaten
11 cups beef or chicken bouillon
1 cup freshly grated parmesan
  cheese

The many and various salami sausages made in every region of Italy are not simple to make. The meats are prepared, sometimes soaked in wine and flavored with various spices, and are then left to age. Some varieties are left to age for about a year in specially prepared ashes. Finally, they are boiled for several hours before serving. You can substitute commercial ravioli for the homemade anolini.

To make the filling, heat the butter in a large saucepan, add the carrot, celery, and onion, and sauté until lightly browned. Add the *cotechino* and the beef. Pour in the bouillon, season with the salt and pepper, then cover tightly and simmer over low heat for 2 to 3 hours, or until the meats are tender and the bouillon has thickened. Remove the saucepan from the heat. Remove the *cotechino* and beef and grind both finely. Place in a bowl with the cooking liquid and set aside until completely cold. Mix in the bread crumbs, cheese, nutmeg, and eggs. Set aside until required.

To make the pasta, lightly beat together the eggs and olive oil in a small bowl. Sift the flour and salt onto a marble slab or into a mixing bowl and make a well in the center. Pour in the eggs and oil, mix to a smooth dough, and knead well. Wrap in a damp cloth and set aside for about 30 minutes. On a lightly floured surface roll the dough into 2 sheets, ¹⁄₁₆ inch thick.

Brush both sheets with the beaten egg. Arrange small balls of the filling, about 1½ inches apart, on the first sheet of dough. Cover with the second sheet and seal by pressing the spaces between the filling with the fingertips. With a fluted cutter or a sharp knife, cut out the *anolini*. Arrange the *anolini* on a lightly floured surface so they do not touch. Bring the bouillon to a boil in a large saucepan and simmer the *anolini* for 8 to 10 minutes, or until they come to the surface. Serve immediately in heated soup dishes with the cheese passed separately.

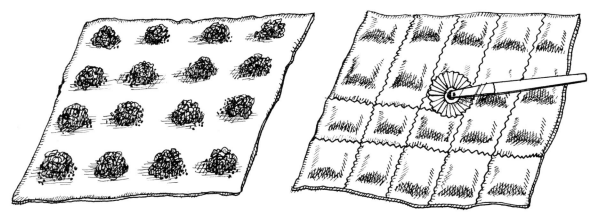

Ricotta-stuffed Pasta

TORTELLONI CON LA RICOTTA

Serves 6

FOR THE PASTA:
2 eggs
1 tb. olive oil
1⅓ cups water, or 3 additional eggs
4 cups all-purpose flour
1 tsp. salt

FOR THE FILLING:
1 lb. ricotta cheese
¼ cup finely minced parsley
½ cup freshly grated parmesan
  cheese
pinch of nutmeg
2 eggs

FOR SERVING:
¾ cup butter
1 cup freshly grated parmesan
  cheese

Deep-fried Veal and Sausage

STECCHI BOLOGNESI

Serves 2 to 3

½ lb. veal or pork tenderloin
6 tbs. butter
½ lb. *mortadella* sausage
¼ lb. parmesan or swiss cheese
2 thick slices bread
warm milk for brushing
all-purpose flour for coating
1 egg
bread crumbs for coating
oil for deep-frying

Tortelloni *are fairly large half-moon–shaped pasta, not to be confused with* tortellini, *which are much smaller semi-circles folded around the tip of the finger so that the 2 ends meet, forming little fat circles.*

To make the pasta, lightly beat together the eggs, olive oil, and water or additional eggs in a small bowl. Sift the flour and salt onto a marble slab or into a mixing bowl and make a well in the center. Pour in the egg mixture, mix to a smooth dough, and knead well. Wrap in a damp cloth and set aside for about 30 minutes.

To make the filling, press the ricotta cheese through a sieve into a bowl. Add the parsley and grated parmesan cheese. Season with the nutmeg and salt and pepper to taste. Mix with the eggs to form a paste. Roll the dough ¹⁄₁₆ inch thick and, using a lightly floured cutter, cut into 3-inch circles. Place 2 teaspoons of the ricotta mixture in the center of each circle, moisten the edges with water, fold over to a half-moon shape, and press the edges to seal.

Cook the *tortelloni*, a few at a time, in a large saucepan half filled with lightly salted boiling water for about 10 minutes, or until they rise to the surface. Remove with a slotted spoon and drain well. Place in a large heated serving dish. Heat the butter to a nut-brown color. Sprinkle the *tortelloni* with the cheese and pour the browned butter on top. Serve immediately.

❧

Because it is easier and less expensive to produce, veal is used more widely than beef in many regions of Italy. The veal that the Italians favor is extremely tender and has a delicate flavor that lends itself well to many types of recipes. This traditional Emilian dish combines quite well with fried artichokes.

Season the veal or pork with salt and pepper. Heat the butter in a skillet, add the veal, and sauté for about 10 minutes, or until tender. Drain well and set aside to cool. Cut into 1-inch cubes. Cut the sausage, cheese, and bread into 1-inch cubes and thread alternately onto long wooden skewers. Brush the skewered ingredients with the milk and sprinkle with flour. Beat the egg with a pinch of salt, brush the ingredients with the egg mixture, and coat with the bread crumbs. Deep-fry in hot oil until golden brown. Drain well and serve hot.

This dish of pasta, layered with poultry and meat sauce and cheese, makes a particularly sustaining meal. You can substitute commercial lasagne for the homemade.

To make the pasta, lightly beat together the eggs and olive oil in a small bowl. Sift the flour and salt onto a marble slab or into a mixing bowl and make a well in the center. Pour in the egg and oil, mix to a smooth dough, and knead well. Wrap in a damp cloth and set aside for 30 minutes.

Roll the dough into 3 sheets, 1/16 inch thick. Cut into 3-inch squares. Cook a few at a time in a large saucepan half filled with lightly salted boiling water for 3 to 5 minutes, or until *al dente.* Remove with a slotted spoon, drain well, and cool on a damp cloth.

Preheat the oven to 350.

To make the sauce, heat the butter in a skillet over moderate heat, add the chicken, and sauté for 2 to 3 minutes. Season with salt and add the Bolognese sauce. Pour half the melted butter into an ovenproof dish and add the pasta in layers, covering each layer with a little of the sauce and a sprinkling of cheese. Sprinkle the top layer with half the grated cheese and the remaining melted butter. Bake in the preheated oven for 40 to 45 minutes and serve with the remaining grated cheese.

Squid, like octopus and cuttlefish, are very popular in Italy.

To clean the squid, carefully remove and discard the transparent bone, the small bladder containing the black ink, and the pouch containing the yellow-colored deposit. Rinse the squid thoroughly in plenty of cold water and pat dry with paper towels. Remove the tentacles and chop them coarsely. Mix together the squid tentacles, garlic, parsley, bread crumbs, half the olive oil, and salt and pepper. Fill the body of each squid with the stuffing.

Preheat the oven to 375.

Sew the body or secure with wooden toothpicks so the filling is completely enclosed. Place the stuffed squid in a greased ovenproof casserole and sprinkle with the remaining olive oil, a little salt and pepper, and the wine. Place the casserole in the preheated oven and bake for 45 to 50 minutes, or until tender. Remove the thread or toothpicks and serve immediately.

Baked Lasagne

LASAGNE PASTICCIATA

Serves 6

FOR THE PASTA:
5 eggs
1 teaspoon olive oil
4 cups all-purpose flour
1 tsp. salt

FOR THE SAUCE:
2 tbs. butter
¾ cup coarsely chopped cooked
　chicken
2 cups Bolognese sauce (see page
　42)
3 tbs. melted butter
1½ cups freshly grated parmesan
　cheese

Baked Stuffed Squid

CALAMARI RIPIENI AL FORNO

Serves 6

3 lbs. fairly large squid
2 cloves garlic, peeled and
　chopped
1 tb. minced parsley
3 tbs. fine fresh breadcrumbs
3 tbs. olive oil
¼ cup dry white wine

Stuffed Capon

CAPPONE RIPIENO

Serves 6

1 capon, about 4 lbs.
1 cup freshly grated stravecchio
  cheese
6 tbs. butter
2 eggs
1 cup fine fresh bread crumbs
3–4 tbs. chicken stock
1 small carrot, scraped
1 small onion, peeled and stuck
  with 1 clove
1 celery stalk

Parmesan cheese, used so extensively in Italian cooking, improves with age and the older cheeses are honored with names of their own—stravecchio for the 3-year-old and stravecchione at 4 years old. This capon is quite good with green sauce.

Using a sharp knife, remove the breastbone from the capon and discard it. Season the cavity of the capon with salt and pepper. Mix together the cheese, butter, eggs, bread crumbs, and salt and pepper to taste, adding enough stock to make a soft stuffing. Fill the bird with the stuffing. Sew the opening and truss the bird with fine string.

Place the capon in a flameproof casserole or a large saucepan and cover with lightly salted cold water. Bring to a boil over moderate heat and carefully skim the surface. Add the carrot, onion, and celery to the pot. Lower the heat, cover tightly, and simmer for about 1½ hours, or until the capon is tender. Remove the capon, drain well, and remove the string. Carve the capon and place on a heated plate.

Italian cooks have devised many utensils for the preparation and shaping of their various pastas. The oldest is the chitarra, *a wooden frame with guitarlike strings or wires. A sheet of dough was pressed through the wires, emerging as flat ribbon noodles. Today this has been mechanized.*

Noodles with Bolognese Sauce

TAGLIATELLE ALLA
BOLOGNESE

Serves 6

5 eggs
1 tsp. olive oil
4 cups all-purpose flour
1 tsp. salt
2 cups Bolognese sauce (see page
  42)
½ cup butter
1 cup freshly grated reggiano
  cheese

Lightly beat together the eggs and olive oil in a small bowl. Sift the flour and salt onto a marble slab or into a mixing bowl and make a well in the center. Pour in the eggs and oil, mix to a smooth dough, and knead well. Wrap in a damp cloth and set aside for about 30 minutes. Roll the dough into two sheets, ¹⁄₁₆ inch thick. Fold each sheet in half lengthwise, then in half again, and, with a sharp knife, cut the dough into noodles ¼ inch wide. Unroll the noodles immediately and leave to dry on a lightly floured surface for 10 to 15 minutes.

Place the *tagliatelle* in a large saucepan half filled with lightly salted boiling water. Simmer for 3 to 5 minutes, or until *al dente*. Remove with a slotted spoon, drain, and place on a heated serving plate. Meanwhile, heat the Bolognese sauce. Cut the butter into small pieces and place on top of the noodles. Cover with half the cheese and half the meat sauce. Bring to the table, mix, and serve immediately with the remaining cheese and meat sauce.

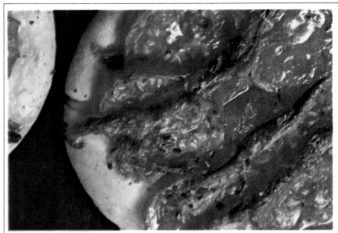

Campania

Campania, the southern region dominated by Naples, is believed to have been settled by the ancient Phoenicians, Cretans, and Greeks. Greek civilization flourished for hundreds of years all along this coastline. In Paestum, south of Naples, are some of the best-preserved Greek architectural monuments, not excepting Greece itself. Today, on the lonely, tranquil plains of the Sele River is a group of ruins of a once-thriving Greek colony founded 600 years before the birth of Christ.

Naples is the gastronomic capital of Campania.

The Neapolitans are gay, relatively poor, and bursting with impudent charm. The same can be said for the cooking: the ingredients are simple, the cooking quick, and the product filled with ingenuity. The region's volcanic soil is extremely fertile.

Because of its fertile volcanic soil, the Romans called the region *campania felix* (the fortunate country). Wheat, corn, and millet grow abundantly and vegetables reach tremendous size. Campanians take advantage of the fertility of the soil: vegetables may grow between rows of widely spaced fruit or olive trees. Frequently three crops are harvested yearly from the same land.

Naples gave birth to *pizzerie*, the pizza shops, and they still proliferate there. The classic *pizza napoletana*, freshly baked for each individual customer, is made with the local mozzarella cheese, anchovies, and, inevitably, olive oil. *Calzone*, the basic pizza dough rolled out until it is paper thin, covered with mozzarella on its own or combined with salami, sprinkled with olive oil, folded over, and baked, is another Neapolitan specialty.

Olive oil, cheese, garlic, and spaghetti are the ingredients of the classic spaghetti *al aglio e olio. Fettuccine alla marinara* are ribbon noodles served with a basil, garlic, and tomato sauce. Round steak, thickly spread with tomato and garlic, is the basis of *bistecca alla pizzaiola.* Other Neapolitan specialties include spaghetti and macaroni *con le vongole,* with clam sauce; or *al sugo,* with meat sauce; or *al pomodoro,* with tomato sauce, of which there are many varieties. The Neapolitan salami lacks delicacy but can be recommended to anyone whose taste buds demand a strident, coarse, heavily seasoned sausage. Its ingredients include pork, beef, and quantities of pepper.

Even vegetable dishes tend to be substantial and pungent. For example, *melanzana,* eggplants, are served with layers of mozzarella and a topping of melted parmesan-type cheese. There are few rice-based dishes in Naples, but *sartu de riso* deserves mention. It consists of meatballs, chicken giblets, mushrooms, peas, cheese, rice, and tomatoes.

The beef from the region is rather inferior, whereas pork and chicken dishes are quite good. Tomatoes are perhaps put to better use in Naples than anywhere else in Italy. A Neapolitan tomato sauce is always delicious, perhaps because the tomatoes are barely cooked instead of being boiled away to a reddish jam as elsewhere. Surprisingly, beyond oysters, there are not many distinctive fish dishes; however, there is a very delicious clam soup, *zuppa di vongole.*

The cooking of Campania is perhaps the spiciest in all of Italy. In *peperoni imbottiti,* red, green, and yellow peppers are baked after being stuffed with a mixture of olives, capers, anchovies, and breadcrumbs.

Sartù is another baked dish; it contains rice, minced veal, chicken giblets, tomatoes, mushrooms, and mozzarella cheese. *Parmigiana di melanzana* has become an international favorite. It appears on restaurant menus here as the well-known eggplant parmigiana.

Bread is an essential item in the region, as it is throughout southern Italy. One of the most traditional Neapolitan dishes is *mozzarella in carrozza,* a fried mozzarella cheese sandwich dipped in flour and beaten egg. And, while speaking of Naples, we dare not forget its ice cream, often said to be the best in the world, and its desserts—*sfogliatelle,* delicious cream, chocolate, or jam-filled pastries; *babà,* a rum cake; *ricottone,* cheese, sugar, and candied citrus peel; and *biscuit tortoni.*

The wines of Campania were praised by Horace and Vergil, but the modern gourmet might think those poets rather overenthusiastic: there may have been odes on Falernian, but the modern Falerno is an undistinguished red or white table wine. Lacrima Christi (tear of Christ), a harsh red or white table wine from the Vesuvian vineyards, is a suitable accompaniment to some of the region's more pungent dishes. Other local wines, lacking eminence but well-suited for daily consumption, include Ravello, Gragnano, and Capri, which is dry and goes well with fish and other seafood.

Tomato and Anchovy Pizza

PIZZA CASALINGA

Serves 6

FOR THE DOUGH:
1 cake or package compressed or
    active dry yeast
1¼ cups lukewarm water
4 cups all-purpose flour
1 tsp. salt
1 tb. olive oil

FOR THE FILLING:
12 anchovy fillets
¼ cup milk
6 tbs. lard
3 large tomatoes (about ¾ lb.),
    peeled and sliced
2 cloves garlic, peeled and sliced
½ tsp. dried oregano

According to historians, the Pompeiians ate pizza. With the arrival of tomatoes in the eighteenth century, pizza became a dish fit for a king. It was, in fact, served by the Bourbons at the Palace of Caserta, and Ferdinand IV had it cooked in the ovens of the famous porcelain factory at Capodimonte.

To make the dough, dissolve the yeast in the water. Sift the flour and salt onto a marble slab or into a mixing bowl and make a well in the center. Pour in the yeast mixture and the olive oil. Knead gradually until you have a smooth, soft dough. Form into a ball and place in a floured bowl. Cover, and let stand in a warm place for 1½ to 2 hours, or until doubled in bulk.

Preheat the oven to 450.

To make the filling, soak the anchovy fillets in the milk for 10 to 15 minutes to remove the excess salt. Drain before using. On a lightly floured surface, knead the risen dough for 2 to 3 minutes. Roll it out to ⅛-inch thickness. Cut into 6 circles, each 6 inches in diameter. Melt the lard and brush a little over each circle. Arrange the anchovy fillets, tomatoes, and garlic over the surface of each. Sprinkle with the oregano and the remaining melted lard and season with salt and pepper. Place on a baking sheet and bake in the preheated oven for 15 to 20 minutes. Remove from the oven and serve immediately.

❦

Clam Soup

ZUPPA DI VONGOLE VERACI

Serves 6

2½ qts. clams
2 cloves garlic
6 tbs. olive oil
½ cup white wine
3¾ cups fish or chicken stock
fried croutons
1 tb. minced parsley

Baby clams are found in the Bay of Naples and are traditionally used in many of the famous fish dishes of the area. A mixture of other shellfish may be substituted if clams are not available.

Thoroughly rinse the clams under cold running water. Peel and crush 1 of the garlic cloves. Heat the olive oil in a large saucepan over moderate heat, add the garlic, and sauté until lightly browned. Pour in the wine, reduce by half, and add the clams and a little pepper. Sauté the clams over high heat, shaking the saucepan occasionally, until they open. Add the stock and bring to a boil.

Peel and halve the remaining garlic clove and rub the cut side around the inside of the soup plates. Place a few croutons in each plate, spoon the clams on top, and pour in the soup. Sprinkle with the parsley and serve immediately.

Marinated Eel

ANGUILLE A SCAPECE

Serves 6

2 lbs. cleaned eel
3 cloves garlic, peeled
all-purpose flour for coating
3 tbs. olive oil
¼ tsp. oregano
¼ fresh chili pepper, chopped,
   or ½ teaspoon dried chili
   powder
1⅓ cups red wine vinegar

Eel is abundant in Italy and is served in many ways. This recipe for eel, served cold or as part of an antipasto plate, is simple to prepare and is particularly tasty. The eel is tenderized by soaking in the marinade, and absorbs its flavor. Many Americans unfamiliar with eel will find this dish an excellent introduction to it.

Rinse the eel under cold running water, dry well, and cut into 2-inch pieces. Cut 1 garlic clove in half and rub the eel with the cut sides. Coat the eel with flour.

Heat the olive oil until very hot, add the eel, and sauté until brown. Drain well and place in an earthenware bowl, in layers, seasoning each layer with the remaining garlic, sliced, oregano, chili pepper, and salt. Pour the vinegar into a saucepan and reduce by one third over high heat. Remove the saucepan from the heat, mix in 3 tablespoons of the frying oil, and pour over the eel. Set aside and marinate for at least 24 hours, but preferably 2 to 3 days to allow the maximum flavor to develop.

Because beef is scarce in Italy it is considered a special treat and is served in many imaginative ways, often with a sauce or marinade. Pizzaiola *sauce is typically Neapolitan, made from fresh tomatoes and flavored with garlic and oregano or basil. It is usually served with meat, but it may be used with fish or pasta.*

Heat the olive oil in a heavy skillet over high heat. Add the steaks and sauté on each side until well browned; then lower the heat and cook for an additional 2 to 3 minutes. Remove the steaks from the skillet and place on a heated plate, sprinkle with salt and pepper, and keep hot.

Add the garlic to the same skillet and sauté over moderate heat until lightly browned. Add the tomatoes and oregano, season with salt, and simmer for about 8 minutes, stirring frequently. Return the steaks and any juices that have drained from them to the skillet and simmer for 3 to 4 minutes. Place the steaks on heated plates, pour a little of the sauce over each, and serve immediately.

Steak with Tomato and Garlic

BISTECCA ALLA PIZZAIOLA

Serves 4

3 tbs. olive oil
4 porterhouse steaks, ¾ inch thick
3 cloves garlic, peeled and crushed
2 medium tomatoes, peeled and
    sliced
dash oregano

Cheese and Salami Turnovers

CALZONE

Serves 6

FOR THE DOUGH:
½ cake or package compressed or active dry yeast
1¼ cups warm water
4 cups all-purpose flour
1 tsp. salt
1 tb. olive oil
1 tb. warm water

FOR THE FILLING:
6 tbs. lard
6 oz. salami, cubed
¾ lb. thinly sliced mozzarella cheese
1 egg, beaten

Calzone are rather like small pizzas but the dough is folded over to enclose the filling. They used to be sold on every street corner and were eaten by farmers and tradespeople alike as they went about their business.

Blend the yeast with the water. Sift the flour and salt onto a marble slab or into a mixing bowl and make a well in the center. Pour in the yeast mixture and the olive oil. Using the fingers, gradually work the flour into the center, adding 1 tablespoon warm water if necessary. Knead until you have a smooth soft dough. Form into a ball and place in a lightly floured bowl. Cover and let stand in a warm place for about 2 hours, or until doubled in bulk.

Preheat the oven to 400.

Knead the risen dough for 2 to 3 minutes on a floured surface. Roll out the dough to ⅛ inch thick and cut into 6 circles, each 6 to 7 inches in diameter. Melt the lard and brush a little over each circle. Arrange the salami and cheese over the surface, leaving a border around the edge. Brush around the edge with the beaten egg and fold each circle in half, pressing the edges lightly together with the fingertips so the filling is completely enclosed. Brush the dough with the remaining lard. Place the *calzone* on a lightly greased baking sheet and bake in the preheated oven for about 20 minutes. Serve immediately.

❦

Deep-fried Open Cheese Sandwich

MOZZARELLA IN CARROZZA

Serves 6

12 anchovy fillets
½ cup warm milk
6 thick slices bread
6 slices mozzarella cheese, the same size and thickness as the bread
2 eggs
all-purpose flour for coating
olive oil and lard for deep-frying

"Mozzarella in a carriage" is a celebrated dish in this region and it is typical of the speedy Neapolitan eating, in which food goes straight from the pan to the mouth! It is another snack sold in the streets and byways of the towns and cities.

Soak the anchovy fillets in half the milk for 10 to 15 minutes to remove the excess salt; then drain. Remove and discard the bread crusts. Place the bread on a flat surface and sprinkle each slice with a little of the remaining milk. Place 2 anchovy fillets on each slice of bread; then cover with a slice of mozzarella. Gently press together to make a neat sandwich.

Lightly beat the eggs with salt and pepper. Coat the sandwiches on each side with flour, dip into the egg, and coat again with flour. Heat the lard and oil together and deep-fry the sandwiches until golden brown. Drain well on paper towels and serve immediately.

Each region of Italy has its own pasta specialties. The Apulians, renowned as the champion pasta eaters in all of Italy, use macaroni in many of their special dishes. This recipe, a flavorful combination of tomatoes, garlic, ham, and cheese served over macaroni, is typical of the region. An important point to remember when cooking pasta of any type is that the water must be boiling rapidly before the pasta is added to the pot. And of course, smaller-sized pasta will require less cooking time than larger sizes.

Break the macaroni into short pieces and cook in plenty of lightly salted boiling water until *al dente*. While it is cooking, make the sauce. Heat the butter and lard in a large skillet over moderate heat. Add the garlic and ham and sauté for 4 to 5 minutes. Add the tomatoes and salt and pepper to taste. Simmer the sauce for 10 to 15 minutes, or until well blended, stirring frequently. When the macaroni is cooked, drain, add the sauce, mix well, and pour into a heated serving dish. Mix the basil with the cheese and sprinkle over the macaroni. Serve immediately.

Macaroni with Tomato, Ham, and Cheese

MACCHERONI
AL SAN GIOVANIELLO

Serves 6

1½ lb. macaroni
3 tbs. butter
3 tbs. lard
3 cloves garlic, peeled and crushed
¼ lb. ground ham
9 large tomatoes (2½ lbs.), peeled and sliced
2–3 tbs. coarsely chopped basil
1 cup freshly grated pecorino cheese

Fava Bean Soup

MINESTRONE DI FAVE FRESCHE

Serves 6

3 lbs. unshelled fresh fava or lima
    beans
½ cup butter
1 small onion, peeled and chopped
1 small carrot, scraped and
    chopped
½ celery stalk, chopped
7½ cups water
4 tsps. salt

FOR THE PASTA:
5 eggs
1 tb. olive oil
4 cups all-purpose flour
1 tsp. salt
1 cup freshly grated pecorino
    cheese

To count the different kinds of minestrone made throughout Italy would be an impossible task. Almost every vegetable grown is used, the soup varying by season and from region to region. You can substitute commercial egg noodles for the homemade pasta.

Shell the beans. Heat the butter in a saucepan over moderate heat, add the onion, carrot, and celery, and sauté until browned. Add the beans and the water. Season with salt and bring to a boil. Lower the heat and simmer the beans for 30 to 40 minutes, or until soft and very tender.

To make the pasta, lightly beat together the eggs and olive oil in a small bowl. Sift the flour and salt onto a marble slab or into a mixing bowl and make a well in the center. Pour in the eggs and oil, mix to a firm, smooth dough, and knead well. Wrap in a damp cloth and set aside for about 30 minutes. Roll the dough on a floured surface into sheets, about 8 inches wide, 12 inches long, and 1/16 inch thick. Fold each sheet in half lengthwise; then in half lengthwise again several times. Cut the roll into ¼-inch ribbon noodles. Unfold the noodles, arrange them on a lightly floured surface, and allow to dry for about 30 minutes.

Bring the soup to a boil and add the egg noodles. Cook for 7 to 8 minutes, or until the noodles are *al dente*. Pour the soup into a tureen and serve with the cheese.

ॐ

Vermicelli with Tomato Sauce

VERMICELLI AL FILETTO DI
POMODORO E BASILICO

Serves 6

6 tablespoons butter
⅓ cup ground ham fat
1 tb. chopped onion
2 large tomatoes (½ lb.), peeled and
    sliced
1½ lb. vermicelli
2–3 tbs. chopped fresh basil
1 cup freshly grated parmesan
    cheese

The literal translation of vermicelli is "little worms." This pasta is similar to spaghetti but thinner.

In a skillet over moderate heat, heat 2 tablespoons of the butter with the ham fat. Add the oinon and sauté until soft and browned; then add the tomatoes. Season with salt and pepper, lower the heat, and simmer gently for 15 minutes, stirring occasionally.

Add the vermicelli to a large saucepan three-fourths full of lightly salted boiling water. Cook rapidly for 3 to 5 minutes, or until *al dente*. Drain and place the vermicelli in a deep heated serving dish. Dot the surface with the remaining butter. Pour over the hot tomato sauce. Sprinkle with the basil and 3 tablespoons of the cheese. Bring to the table; then toss the ingredients to mix. Pass the remaining cheese separately.

Tuscany

Florence, city of the Medicis, Machiavelli, Boccaccio, Michelangelo, Giotto, and Dante; Siena, where horses race in the main square; and Pisa of the leaning tower: these are just some of Tuscany's attractions. But to the winebidder, Tuscany is the home of Chianti, best known of all Italian wines. Chianti, which comes in the characteristic straw-covered flasks, is available in white or red. Only when it comes from the region between Florence and Siena may it bear the official yellow seal that entitles it to be sold as Chianti Classico. Tuscany produces about a hundred million gallons of wine a year, almost all of it very acceptable. Montepulciano, Mont Albano, and Pomino are thoroughly honest red table wines. The white Santa Christine is agreeably delicate and flowery. Most Tuscan wines are drunk young. If matured for two years, they qualify as *vecchio*, or old wine. *Stravecchio* is wine that has been matured for three years or more.

Aside from its wine, Tuscany is also the home of excellent olive oil, meat, vegetables, and good plain cooking. Indeed, compared to the rest of Italy, its cuisine is considered to be the most traditional in nature, relatively unaffected by outside influences. Sauces, spices, and herbs play little part in the Tuscan cuisine, and their cooking is characterized by an avoidance of unnecessary detail and careful attention to the selection of the finest raw materials. The renowned *costata fiorentina* is simply an enormous steak grilled over charcoal, the only allowable additives being salt, pepper, and a little olive oil. Many people consider this the very best meal that can be had in Florence. This is due in large measure to the Chianina breed of cattle. It is probably the oldest as well as the tallest and heaviest breed of beef cattle in the world. The breed goes back centuries and was prized by the Romans for tenderness. The Chianinas are remarkable for quick growth and great weight. A year-old bull weighs over 1,000 pounds; a 2-year-old may go over a ton. The flesh of the Chianinas is virtually without fat and with an exceptionally high percentage of meat concentrated in the choicer cuts. In its simplicity, Chianina beefsteak is the most famous dish of Florence.

Chickens, mainly of the local Leghorn breed, are also cooked very simply: brushed with olive oil and broiled whole. Sometimes the breasts are gently fried without herbs or salt or pepper or, as in *pollo alla diavola alla fiorentina*, grilled with a deviled sauce. These dishes depend on free-range chickens that have an intrinsic flavor of their own.

Crostini di fegatini, an excellent dish of ham, chicken livers, and croutons, is often served as a first course, as is *ravioli e gnocchi verdi*, a spinach-based *gnocchi* dish. Other first courses are *fagioli toscana col tonno* (white beans and tuna fish) and the Florentine white bean soup, *zuppa di fagioli alla fiorentina*. *Fagioli al fiasco* (beans in a flask) is a very famous vegetable dish, cooked in a wine flask. In fact, beans play a dominant role in the Tuscan diet and can usually be found as part of a dish on any stage of their menu except dessert. Other popular regional specialties include *minestrone di fagioli* (bean soup with tomatoes and celery) and *riso e fagioli* (rice and beans).

Apart from their excellent home-raised beef, pork, and poultry, Tuscans are avid eaters of small birds, some, such as figpeckers, unknown in other parts of Europe. These birds, as well as quail and snipe, are usually roasted in oil and eaten with bread fried in the pan juices. They also relish the excellent trout, chestnuts, walnuts, melons, and small game from the town of Arezzo. The coastal town of Grosseto provides some fine fish, especially eel, as well as a variety of game, including rabbit, deer, and wild boar. Excellent game is also found on the island of Elba, which also offers an abundance of fresh seafood, including lobster and octopus. An elaborate Tuscan dish is *cacciuocco livornese*, the rich Leghorn fish soup made from a selection of fish and shellfish, garlic, onions, sage, tomatoes, and white wine. *Salame fiorentina* is the regional sausage, made of pure pork. *Finocchiona* is a popular variety of sausage that contains fennel seeds. And a favorite Tuscan snack, which typifies the simplicity of the regional cooking, is *bruschetta:* slices of white bread baked in the oven until they are crisp and golden, rubbed with garlic, and eaten with the limpid, fruity Tuscan olive oil, accompanied by copious draughts of Tuscan wine.

The town of Lucca serves the region with an array of delicious desserts and sweets. A traditional favorite is *buccellato*, a cake made of flour, sugar, vanilla, raisins, and aniseed accompanied by strawberries marinated in sugared wine. Another favorite dessert, one enjoyed in Lucca as well as other Tuscan areas, is *cenci*—literally "tatters." The name refers to the rather informal appearance of these strips of pastry dough, which are tied in knots or bows, and are deep fried.

Meat Sauce

SUGO DI CARNE

Makes 2½ cups

¼ lb. pork or ham rind
1 lb. rolled rump of beef
¼ lb. ham or Canadian bacon,
   chopped into ½-inch cubes
3 tbs. ground ham
2 tsps. salt
¼ tsp. pepper
2 medium carrots, scraped and
   sliced
1 medium onion, peeled and
   chopped (about ¾ cup)
1 clove garlic, peeled and chopped
1 celery stalk, chopped
3 dried mushrooms, soaked,
   drained and chopped, or 3 fresh
   mushrooms, chopped
1 clove
bouquet garni
⅓ cup dry red wine
¼ cup all-purpose flour
1 large tomato, peeled and
   chopped
3¾ cups hot water

The practical Italian housewife shows her ingenuity in preparing this recipe since it may be used for both a main meat dish and a sauce for pasta. It is included in many of the recipes in this book. You can double this recipe and freeze the sauce for future use.

Blanch the pork rind in boiling water for 5 minutes. Drain well and chop coarsely. Make small incisions in the beef and insert a cube of ham or bacon into each. Sprinkle the beef with salt and pepper.

Preheat the oven to 300.

Place the pork rind and ground ham in an ovenproof casserole. Sauté over low heat until the fat begins to melt. Place the beef in the casserole with the carrots, onion, garlic, celery, mushrooms, and clove. Increase the heat to moderate and sauté the ingredients until the beef begins to brown. Add the bouquet garni of 1 bay leaf, 1 sprig thyme, and 1 sprig marjoram, and the wine. Increase the heat and boil rapidly until the wine is reduced almost completely. Remove the saucepan from the heat and stir in the flour. Return to moderate heat and simmer for 2 to 3 minutes, stirring constantly. Stir in the tomatoes and the water. Bring to a boil. Remove the saucepan from the heat, cover tightly, and cook in the preheated oven for 4 hours.

Remove the beef from the casserole and use in another dish. Press the sauce through a sieve into a saucepan. Place over moderate heat and simmer gently until reduced to a consistency thick enough to coat the back of a spoon. Adjust the seasoning and skim the surface to remove any fat. Pour the sauce into a bowl and set aside to cool. Use as required. This meat sauce can be kept for several days in the refrigerator.

bouquet garni

Noodles in Hare Sauce

PAPPARDELLE CON LA LEPRE

Serves 6

3 lbs. hare pieces

FOR THE MARINADE:
½ small onion, peeled
½ celery stalk, sliced
1 bay leaf, crumbled
2 cups full-bodied red wine
2 peppercorns

FOR THE PASTA:
4 eggs
1 tb. olive oil
4 cups all-purpose flour
1 tsp. salt

FOR THE SAUCE:
1 tb. olive oil
½ onion, peeled and chopped
½ carrot, scraped and chopped
2 slices Canadian bacon, chopped
pinch of nutmeg
chicken stock
¼ cup butter

The valleys and wooded hills of Tuscany provide excellent shooting ground for small-game hunters. Hare is hung for several days before being prepared in this traditional Tuscan way.

Rinse the hare pieces under cold running water and dry with a cloth or paper towels.

To make the marinade, place the onion, celery, and bay leaf in a glass or enamel bowl with the wine and peppercorns. Add the hare and set aside to marinate for several hours, turning occasionally.

To make the pasta, lightly beat together the eggs and olive oil in a small bowl. Sift the flour and salt onto a marble slab or into a mixing bowl and make a well in the center. Pour in the eggs and the oil, mix to a firm, smooth dough, and knead well. Wrap in a damp cloth and set aside for about 30 minutes.

Roll the dough on a floured surface to about 1/16 inch thick. With a sharp knife, cut the dough into _pappardelle_ about ¼ inch wide. Set aside on a floured surface to dry.

To make the sauce, heat the oil in a skillet over moderate heat, add the onion, carrot, and bacon, and sauté until lightly browned. Drain and dry the pieces of hare, season with salt and nutmeg, place in the skillet, and sauté until browned. Lower the heat and cook gently for about 1 hour, or until tender, occasionally adding 1 tablespoon of the marinade and 1 tablespoon of the stock to form a thin sauce. Remove the pieces of hare and strain the sauce through a fine sieve. Keep both hot. Place the _pappardelle_ in a large saucepan half filled with lightly salted boiling water. Simmer for 8 to 12 minutes, or until _al dente_. Drain and pour into a deep heated serving dish. Cover with the sauce and place small pieces of the butter on the surface. Bring to the table, mix well, and serve immediately.

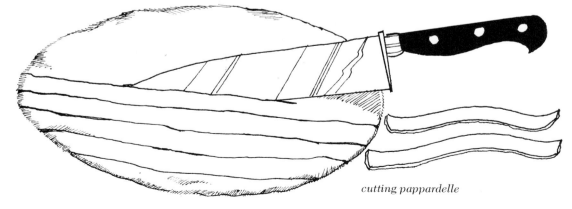

cutting pappardelle

Tripe, preferably the finer veal tripe, is a specialty of Italy.

Split the calf's foot in half lengthwise. Clean and rinse thoroughly under cold running water. Stick one onion with the cloves. Place the calf's foot in a large saucepan with the salt and cover with water. Add the tripe, the onion stuck with the cloves, and the celery. Place over high heat and bring to a boil. Lower the heat and simmer for 1 hour.

Remove the tripe with a slotted spoon and set aside until required. Continue cooking the pieces of calf's foot for an additional 45 minutes to 1 hour, or until tender. Remove the saucepan from the heat, take out the calf's foot, and cool. Cut the flesh into ½-inch strips. Reserve the stock.

Chop the remaining onion. Heat the butter and olive oil in a saucepan, add the onion and the ham fat, and sauté until lightly browned. Add the meat sauce. Stir for a few minutes; then add the tripe and calf's foot. Simmer for 3 to 4 minutes, adding 3 to 4 tablespoons of the reserved stock, if necessary, to prevent the meat from sticking. Season with the pepper. Pour into a deep, heated serving dish, sprinkle with the marjoram and cheese, and serve hot.

Florentine Tripe and Calf's Foot

TRIPPA E ZAMPA
ALLA FIORENTINA

Serves 6

1 calf's foot
2 medium onions, peeled
2 cloves
1 tsp. salt
2 lbs. precooked tripe
1 celery stalk
½ cup butter
3 tbs. olive oil
3 tbs. finely ground ham fat
1¼ cups meat sauce (see page 64)
¼ teaspoon marjoram
¾ cup freshly grated parmesan
   cheese

Braised Veal

GRILLETTATO DI VITELLO
ALLA TOSCANA

Serves 6

¼ lb. boiled ham
2 lbs. rolled leg of veal
flour for coating
3 tbs. butter
3 tbs. olive oil
1 medium onion, peeled and
    chopped (about ¾ cup)
⅔ cup dry red wine
2 medium potatoes, peeled
1 lemon
1 clove garlic, peeled
pinch of nutmeg

Tuscan cooking makes good use of its excellent local wines, and the wine-growers of the area concentrate on producing different varieties. Chianti, which is almost synonymous with Tuscany, is a very suitable wine for this dish.

Cut the ham into thin strips. Wipe the veal with a damp cloth or paper towels. Tie the veal with fine string to maintain its shape, season with salt and pepper, and lightly coat with flour. Heat the butter and olive oil in a casserole over high heat, add the veal, and sauté until browned on all sides. Add the onion and sauté until golden brown; then add the ham. Pour in the wine gradually and reduce it almost completely. Add water to barely cover the meat, cover the casserole tightly, and, stirring occasionally, simmer for 1¼ to 1½ hours, or until the veal is tender. Place the potatoes in a saucepan, cover with water, and cook until tender; then drain well.

Meanwhile, finely pare the lemon rind. Chop the garlic with the lemon rind. A few minutes before removing the casserole from the heat, add the potatoes, garlic, lemon rind, and nutmeg. Remove the veal from the casserole, carve into slices, and place on a heated serving plate. Cover with the sauce, garnish with the potatoes, and serve.

Although frogs are not fish, the most likely place to buy them is at the fish market.

If using frozen frogs' legs, thaw and drain them well. Season the frogs' legs with salt and pepper. Heat 1 tablespoon of the olive oil in a heavy skillet over moderate heat, add the onion, and sauté until lightly browned. Add the frogs' legs and sauté until browned on each side. Remove the skillet from the heat, strip the flesh from the frogs' legs, and set aside to cool.

Beat the eggs and stir in the frog flesh. Pour the remaining oil into the skillet with the onion and cook until very hot over high heat. Add the egg mixture and, using a fork, stir briskly; then allow the mixture to set slightly. Lower the heat to allow the eggs to cook more slowly so they thicken evenly and smoothly. When the mixture begins to set, shake the skillet to loosen the omelet from the bottom. Loosen the edges, using a fork or a spatula. Turn the omelet over and cook the other side. Serve immediately on a heated serving plate.

Frogs' Legs Omelet

FRITTATA DI RANE

Serves 6

24 pairs fresh or frozen frogs' legs
6 tbs. olive oil
1 tb. chopped onion
10 eggs

The white flesh of the frogs' legs is the edible part. It is tender, delicate, and delicious, not unlike chicken flesh.

Wild boar, which is still available in Italy, is traditionally used in this magnificent Tuscan recipe. Since boar is unfamiliar to Americans, and generally unavailable in this country, a rolled pork loin roast should be substituted.

Wash the meat and dry it with paper towels. To make the marinade, place the onions, garlic, carrot, wine, vinegar, celery, cloves, peppercorns, and bay leaf in a saucepan. Bring to the simmering point and remove immediately from the heat. Let stand until cold. Place the meat in a deep glass bowl.

Pour the marinade over the meat and set aside to marinate for 2 days, turning two or three times a day.

Drain the meat, dry it carefully with a cloth or paper towels, and tie with string into a neat shape. Sprinkle the meat with salt and pepper. Soak the white raisins and prunes in a little warm water until plump. Heat the lard in a saucepan over high heat. Add the meat and sauté until brown on all sides. Add the onions, carrot, celery, and cloves. Crumble the thyme and add with the bay leaf, prosciutto, and bacon fat. Continue turning the meat and stirring the other ingredients during the cooking until everything is well browned. Pour in the wine and, using a wooden spoon, loosen the brown sediment at the bottom of the pan. Reduce the wine almost completely and barely cover the meat with cold water. Lower the heat, cover tightly, and cook over very low heat for 1½ to 2 hours, or until the meat is tender and the sauce is a thick pouring consistency.

Remove the meat from the saucepan, untie it, place on a heated plate, cover with a few tablespoons of the sauce, and keep hot. Strain the remaining sauce through a fine sieve into a bowl. Put the garlic into a saucepan and add the ½ bay leaf, sugar, and water. Place over low heat and stir constantly to dissolve the sugar. Remove saucepan from the heat and, when slightly cooled, add the chocolate and stir until melted. Pour in the vinegar and reduce it by half over high heat; then add the strained sauce from the meat. If the sauce is not sufficiently thick, stir in the potato flour or cornstarch, blended with a little cold water. Remove and discard the pits from the prunes and cherries, and cut the flesh into small pieces. Chop the citron. Add the drained white raisins, prunes, cherries, citron, and pignolia nuts to the sauce. Reheat the sauce. Carve the meat into slices and arrange on a heated serving dish. Pour on the hot sauce and serve immediately.

Wild Boar in Sweet and Sour Sauce

CINGHIALE IN AGRODOLCE

Serves 6

3 lbs. wild boar or rolled pork loin roast

FOR THE MARINADE:
2 small onions, peeled
1 clove garlic, peeled
1 small carrot, scraped
¾ cup dry white wine
6 tbs. vinegar
½ celery stalk
2 cloves
4 peppercorns
1 bay leaf

FOR THE SAUCE:
2 tbs. seedless white raisins
6 prunes
¼ cup lard
2 small onions, peeled and sliced (about 1 cup)
1 small carrot, scraped and sliced
1 celery stalk, sliced
2 cloves
pinch of thyme
1 small bay leaf
¼ lb. prosciutto, diced (½ cup)
¼ cup diced bacon fat
¾ cup dry white wine
1 clove garlic, peeled and crushed
½ bay leaf, crumbled
3 tbs. sugar
1 tb. water
4 tbs. grated cooking chocolate
6 tbs. vinegar
2 tsps. potato flour or cornstarch
12 Bing cherries
¼ cup candied citron or orange peel, chopped
¼ cup pignolia nuts

Deviled Chicken

POLLO ALLA DIAVOLA ALLA
FIORENTINA

Serves 6

1 4-lb. chicken
⅔ cup olive oil
few sprigs parsley
2–3 sprigs rosemary
1 clove garlic, peeled and crushed
juice of 1 lemon

In Tuscany, farmers raise small, tender, plump chickens that until recently were considered a luxury food to be served only on special occasions. In this recipe, delicate herbs and a faint touch of garlic are combined with the chicken to produce a unique flavor that is further enhanced by grilling over a charcoal or wood fire. If the chicken is to be oven broiled, reduce cooking time by 10 minutes.

Split the chicken along the backbone but do not cut it completely in half. Open out and lightly beat it with a meat mallet or wood rolling pin so it remains flat. Remove and discard as many bones as possible. Place the chicken in a bowl with olive oil, parsley, rosemary, salt, and pepper. Crush the garlic and squeeze the lemon. Add the garlic and lemon juice to the chicken and set it aside to marinate for about 1 hour.

Cook the chicken over the hot embers of a charcoal fire until golden brown on each side. Move the chicken farther away from the source of heat and cook for an additional 40 to 45 minutes, or until tender. During the cooking, turn the chicken frequently and brush with the marinade.

Olive oil is a source of pride in this region. Each season the Tuscans take their home-grown olives to be pressed locally and made into their favorite oil.

Remove and discard any membrane and white fatty parts from the liver. Rinse the liver under cold running water and pat dry with a cloth or paper towels. Cut the liver into 1½- to 2-inch pieces.

Mix the garlic with the bread crumbs. Soak the pork caul in warm water until it is soft and pliable. Drain well and cut into rectangles, about 5 inches by 2 inches. Place the caul on a flat surface and sprinkle with salt, pepper, and the bread crumb mixture.

Wrap each piece of liver in a piece of caul and thread onto long metal skewers, alternating with bay leaves and cubes of bread. Brush with olive oil and cook on a spit over glowing charcoal or cook under a moderately hot broiler for 10 to 15 minutes, or until well browned and tender. Serve immediately with the cheese.

Grilled Liver

FAGATELLI DI MAIALE ALLA FIORENTINA

Serves 6

1 lb. pork liver
2 cloves garlic, peeled and finely chopped
2 cups dry bread crumbs
¾ lb. pork caul
bay leaves
4 thick slices bread, cubed
olive oil
1 cup freshly grated parmesan cheese

Beans in a Flask

FAGIOLI AL FIASCO

Serves 6

2 cups navy beans
2 cloves garlic, peeled and crushed
6 tbs. olive oil
few fresh or dried sage leaves

This very famous Tuscan dish is cooked in a wine flask so that no flavor will escape. Traditionally, the beans were cooked outside over smoldering charcoal embers.

Clean the beans and soak them in plenty of cold water for at least 12 hours. Drain and place in a Chianti flask from which the straw has been removed. The flask should be about three quarters full so the beans can swell. Add the garlic, olive oil, and sage and cover with water. Plug the flask loosely with straw or cotton wool so the steam can escape during cooking and help the beans absorb the oil.

Place the flask over the glowing embers of a charcoal fire or in an oven preheated to 375. Cook for 3 hours. Pour beans into a serving bowl and season with a little more olive oil and salt and pepper to taste. Serve hot.

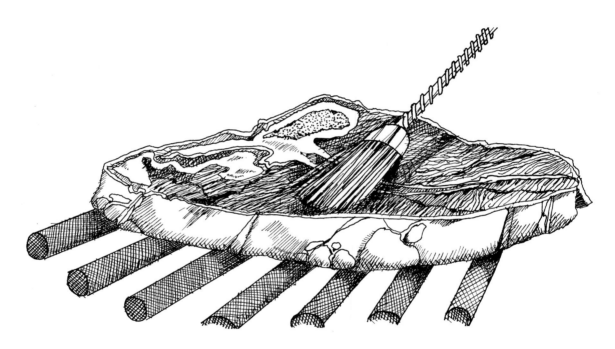

Florentine Grilled Steaks

COSTATA FIORENTINA

Serves 6

6 T-bone steaks
3 tbs. olive oil

Chianina steers are generally killed at about 15 months. The choice, red, fatless meat is hung for several days. Each steak contains a generous portion of the fillet still attached.

Brush both sides of each steak with olive oil and sprinkle with pepper. Set aside to marinate for about 10 minutes. Grill according to individual taste over a charcoal fire, if possible, or cook under a hot broiler. Season with salt. In Tuscany the steaks are served rare and brushed with the remaining olive oil just before serving.

Pork with Cardoons

ARISTA DI MAIALE CON CARDI

Serves 6

¼ tsp. rosemary
¼ tsp. sage
2 lbs. rolled pork loin roast
¼ cup butter
1 clove garlic, peeled and crushed
3 tbs. chopped onion
6 tbs. dry white wine
2 lbs. cardoons or 2 bunches celery
¼ cup ground ham
5 large tomatoes (1 lb.), peeled and
   chopped

> Cardoons, like artichokes, are
> members of the thistle family—
> though the tender stalks and
> roots are eaten rather than the
> flower. When preparing car-
> doons, discard the outside stalks
> and trim the strings, as for pre-
> paring celery.

The cardoon is a vegetable of the thistle family.

Crush the rosemary and sage to a powder. Rub the pork with the herbs, season with salt and pepper, and tie into a neat shape with fine string.

Heat half the butter in a saucepan over moderate heat, add the garlic and half the onion, and sauté until golden brown. Add the pork and sauté for 5 minutes on all sides, or until well browned. Pour in the wine and reduce it almost completely; then lower the heat, cover tightly, and simmer for 45 minutes. During this time, baste the pork frequently adding hot water, if necessary.

Meanwhile, clean the cardoons, wash under running water, and cut into small pieces. Place the cardoons in salted boiling water and simmer for 5 to 10 minutes. Drain well. Heat the remaining butter in a saucepan over moderate heat, add the ham and the remaining onion, and sauté until lightly browned. Add the tomatoes. Season with salt and pepper and cook for about 20 minutes. Strain the tomato sauce through a fine sieve into a second saucepan. Add the cardoons and simmer over moderate heat for 5 minutes. Untie the loin of pork, carve into slices, and arrange on a heated serving plate. Surround with the cardoons in the tomato sauce and serve immediately.

Deep-fried Pastries

CENCI ALLA FIORENTINA

Serves 6

3 cups all-purpose flour
¼ cup butter
3 eggs
pinch of sugar
oil for deep-frying
vanilla sugar or confectioners
   sugar for coating

These fried Tuscan pastries can be served alone or with a cold dessert.

Sift the flour onto a marble surface or into a mixing bowl and make a well in the center. Cream the butter until soft, then place the butter, eggs, sugar, and a pinch of salt in the well, mix to a dough, and knead until all the flour has been absorbed. Continue kneading until the pastry is smooth and firm. Wrap in a lightly floured cloth and set aside in a cool place for about 1 hour.

Place the dough on a floured surface and cut into 2 or 3 pieces. Roll each piece into a sheet, about ⅛ inch thick, and cut into circles, rectangles, or strips.

Heat the oil until very hot and fry the *cenci*, a few at a time, until golden brown. Drain well and sprinkle with sugar. Serve on a round plate lined with a paper napkin.

Apulia, Lucania, and Calabria

These are the southernmost provinces of Italy. Apulia forms the heel of Italy's boot, Lucania the instep, and Calabria the toe. Dire poverty reigned here until a few years ago. There were practically no roads, and mosquitoes attacked everything that moved. A revolution has been brought about by irrigation, drainage schemes, and superb new roads. The tourist industry is, today, the main means of support. This is largely due to the fact that the Calabrian coastal resorts boast about 345 days of sunshine every year.

In Calabria, specifically the region around the city of Reggio Calabria, 40,000 acres are planted with citrus trees, over 6 million of them, which produce 135,000 tons of fruit annually. One citrus fruit raised here is the bergamot; it is never eaten because it is worth too much as an essential element in perfume. The bergamot looks like a large lemon and Reggio Calabria has a world monopoly on its oil. The entire supply comes from there and attempts to grow the fruit elsewhere have been unsuccesful. This monopoly is very significant in the economy of Calabria since the sale of bergamot oil brings in millions of dollars every year.

An enormous range of vegetables is grown here, including artichokes, asparagus, eggplants, celery, and the sweet peppers and tomatoes which make the famous *peperonata.* Eggplant is featured in *melanzana ripiene* (stuffed with anchovy, olives, garlic, and capers, sprinkled with breadcrumbs, and then baked) and *melanzana al funghetto* (fried, chopped eggplant with oil, garlic, parsley, and pepper). There is a lot of game, and pigs and goats are reared domestically.

The Ionian Sea provides fish and excellent oysters and mussels, hence *tiella alla pugliese* (mussel hot-pot) and *cozze alla marinara* (mussels with white wine and garlic). *Zuppa di pesce* is the local version of the French *bouillabaisse;* its Apulian incarnation is a hearty fish stew with spices, garlic, tomatoes, and herbs. *Capitone* (fried eel), *cozze gratinate* (mussels in oil, parsley, garlic, and breadcrumbs), and *trote arrostite* (barbecued or roasted spiced trout) are further examples of the ingenious way the region's cooks take advantage of the sea's bounty.

Many local meat dishes depend on pork products. There is a good *capocollo* (smoked salt pork) and a wide variety of sausages, for which Lucania is particularly noted. *Soppressata* are made of pig's head with pistachio nuts. A feature of feast days is *capretto ripieno al forno* (oven-baked stuffed kid). One unusual dish is *mazzacorde,* which consists of blanched sheep's intestines, fried with garlic, oregano, parsley, and peppers.

The region produces no really great cheese, but a wide range of good ones. There are many versions of pecorino, a hard ewes'-milk cheese, much used as a condiment and for cooking. Genuine mozzarella, produced from buffaloes' milk, is still made in Apulia and Calabria, as is provola, a smoked buffaloes'-milk cheese. The Calabrian butirro is unique: it is a hard cheese, the size and shape of a pear, made from either buffaloes' or cows' milk, enclosing an egg of fresh butter.

Fine desserts come from Apulia and Calabria. There's *turiddu,* biscuits made from flour, eggs, and white wine, then fried in oil, soaked in honey and coated with sugar or chocolate; *mostaccioli,* cookies shaped in designs of hearts, fish, etc.; *cartellate,* ribbons of sweet dough soaked in honey. In Lucania, lightly roasted figs, stuffed with fennel seeds and almonds and then roasted a little more, is a popular dessert. One curious dessert is *pizza rustica,* which is puff paste stuffed with grapes, sweet ricotta cheese, and sweetened salami, eaten hot from the oven.

Apulia was at one time Italy's major wine-producing province, in quantity if not quality (but it has now been overtaken by Veneto). Here are produced the *vini da taglio,* or blending wines, which are used to reinforce the more effete wines of the north in the production of modest table wines. San Severe, which comes as either red or white, is an above-average local table wine, and Locorotondo, a good dry white, can also be recommended. Many Apulian white wines are used in the manufacture of vermouth. Lucania produces good dry red wines from the Aglianico grape in the Vulture and Insina districts. They are *pétillants* and have a delicate flavor of raspberries that masks a high alcoholic content. Aglianico del Vulture is particularly recommended. Calabria produces some trustworthy red wines, among which should be mentioned Cirò, which is rather sweet, and Lacrima di Castrovillari, which is rather dry.

Mussel Hot Pot

TIELLA DI COZZE

Serves 6

2 qts. mussels
3 tbs. olive oil
¼ tsp. coarsely ground pepper
½ cup ground bacon fat
1 small onion, peeled and minced
1 clove garlic, peeled and minced
9 cups cold water
4 medium potatoes, peeled and
    sliced (3½–4 cups)
1¾ cups plain uncooked rice

> Mussels deteriorate rapidly and can be the cause of infection. To test mussels for freshness, try to slide the two halves of the shell across each other. If they budge, the shell is probably filled with mud, and the mollusk should be discarded.

The city of Taranto, located between a coastal lagoon and a salt-water gulf, is ideally situated for the cultivation of oysters, mussels, and other mollusks. The shellfish are raised in the center of the city in the Mar Grande, where they are allowed to mature for up to eighteen months before harvesting. The tiella, *distantly related to the Spanish* paella, *is a dish built up of layers of different ingredients.*

Scrub the mussels thoroughly under running water, brushing them to remove seaweed, sand, and grit. Remove the beards. Heat half the olive oil in a saucepan over moderate heat. Add the mussels and pepper and sauté until the mussels open. Shake the saucepan frequently to prevent the mussels from sticking. Drain them in a colander over a large bowl and cool. Strain and reserve the liquid. Remove and discard the mussel shells. Discard any mussels that haven't opened. Set the mussels aside.

Heat the bacon fat and the remaining olive oil in a flame-proof casserole or a saucepan over low heat. Add the onion and garlic and sauté until lightly browned. Add the water and the potatoes, season with salt, and bring to a boil. After 10 minutes, add the rice and cook over high heat for 15 to 20 minutes. Add the mussels and the reserved liquid 2 to 3 minutes before the end of the cooking time. Pour into a heated serving dish and serve immediately.

Mussels with White Wine and Garlic

COZZE ALLA MARINARA

Serves 6

4 qts. mussels
6 tbs. olive oil
6 cloves garlic, peeled and sliced
½ chili pepper
6 tbs. dry white wine
1 tb. minced parsley

This is a fairly well-known method of cooking mussels, similar to the French moules marinières. *It is important not to overcook the mussels since this makes them tough. A freshly baked, crusty Italian bread served with sweet butter and a well-chilled white wine makes this dish a complete meal.*

Scrub the mussels thoroughly under running water, brushing them to remove seaweed, sand, and grit. Remove the beards. Heat the olive oil in a large saucepan, add the garlic and chili pepper, and sauté until browned. Add the mussels with the wine and parsley. Simmer until the mussels have opened, shaking the pan frequently. Add a few tablespoons of warm water, if necessary, to prevent the mussels from sticking. Discard any mussels that haven't opened. Serve immediately.

Lamb Fricassee

AGNELLO IN FRICASSEA

Serves 6

2 lbs. rolled leg or shoulder of lamb
3 tbs. olive oil
1 small onion, peeled and chopped
¼ cup ground ham
pinch of nutmeg
¾ cup dry white wine
2 tbs. all-purpose flour
2 cloves garlic, peeled
few sprigs parsley
4 egg yolks
3 tbs. lemon juice

Lamb Stew

RAGÙ DI AGNELLO
CON PATATE

Serves 6

2 lbs. shoulder of lamb
1 tb. olive oil
½ cup ground bacon fat
½ small carrot, scraped and
   minced
½ onion, peeled and minced
1 clove garlic, peeled and minced
1 celery stalk, peeled and minced
⅔ cup dry white wine
¾ cup tomato sauce (see page 43)
¾ cup water
¼ tsp. chili powder
3 medium potatoes, peeled and
   diced (about 3 cups)

In the hills, lamb is cooked in numerous ways. This fricassee with its egg and lemon sauce is one of the more refined, subtly flavored dishes.

Cut the lamb into 1½-inch cubes. Heat the olive oil in a casserole or skillet over moderate heat. Add the lamb, onion, ham, nutmeg, salt, and pepper and stir constantly. When the meat begins to brown, add the wine and reduce it to 1 tablespoon. Sprinkle in the flour and mix thoroughly. Stir in enough water to barely cover the lamb. Simmer over low heat for 50 to 60 minutes, or until the lamb is tender. During the cooking, if necessary, add a few tablespoons of water to prevent the meat from sticking.

Chop the garlic with the parsley. Stir the garlic mixture into the casserole 2 to 3 minutes before the end of the cooking time. Remove the casserole from the heat.

Lightly beat the egg yolks with the lemon juice, and slowly blend into the liquid in the casserole. Replace over the heat until the mixture is hot and the sauce thickens, but do not boil. Remove the casserole from the heat and pour the fricassee into a deep heated serving dish. Serve immediately.

❧

This recipe, with white wine, tomato sauce, and potatoes, has become a typical way of cooking lamb. With slight regional variations, it appears throughout Italy, and indeed throughout the whole Mediterranean area.

Cut the lamb into 1½-inch cubes. Heat the olive oil in a flameproof casserole or a saucepan over high heat, add the lamb, and sauté until browned. Remove the lamb from the casserole and set aside.

Add the bacon fat, carrot, onion, garlic, and celery to the casserole. Sauté until browned, then pour in the wine, and reduce to ¼ cup over high heat. Add the tomato sauce diluted with the water, season lightly with chili powder and salt, and simmer gently over moderate heat for 15 minutes. Return the lamb to the casserole and simmer for an additional 20 to 30 minutes, stirring frequently, until the lamb is tender. Meanwhile, place the potatoes in a saucepan, cover with water, bring to a boil, and simmer until almost cooked. Drain well and add to the lamb about 10 minutes before the end of the cooking time.

Pepper and Tomato Stew

PEPERONATA

Serves 6

½ cup olive oil
1 large onion, peeled and coarsely
    chopped (1 scant cup)
2–3 cloves garlic, peeled and sliced
6 bay leaves
6 medium sweet peppers (2 lbs.),
    seeded and chopped
6 large tomatoes (1½ lbs.), peeled,
    or 2 (1 lb.) cans tomatoes,
    drained

This vegetable dish is an excellent appetizer or first course. It can be prepared in advance and reheated.

Heat the olive oil in a skillet over moderate heat. Add the onion, garlic, and bay leaves and sauté until golden brown. Add the sweet peppers and season with salt and pepper. Cook over high heat for about 10 minutes, stirring constantly. Add the tomatoes, lower the heat, and simmer gently for an additional 15 minutes. Pour into a heated serving dish and serve immediately.

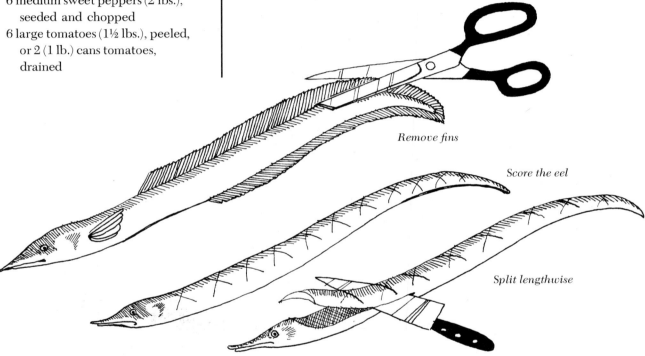

Remove fins

Score the eel

Split lengthwise

Broiled Eels

ANGUILLA COTTA SULLA
GRATICOLA

Serves 6

2 lbs. small or medium eels
olive oil (optional)
3 lemons, wedged

This dish is often eaten with large chunks of bread. A specialty of the Calabria area, bread is still made in huge round loaves, big enough to last a family for a week and weighing up to 20 pounds.

Remove and discard the fins from each eel. Score across each eel with a sharp knife several times and split open lengthwise from the head to the tail. Remove and discard the intestines and the backbone. Wash and dry the flesh thoroughly; then season with salt. Brush with a little olive oil unless the eels are very fatty, and cook under a hot broiler for 10 to 15 minutes, turning frequently, until the flesh is firm and tender. Serve the eels on a heated serving plate with the lemon wedges.

Veneto

Although still magnificent, Venice in medieval days was one of the wealthiest and most brilliant cities in the world. The bulk of its riches came from the importing, and subsequent sale to the rest of Europe, of what were at that time rare foods. Included were sugar, spices, coffee, salt, and pepper. Naturally, Venice itself made considerable use of these products, and thus developed one of the finest cuisines of all Europe, characteristically hot and spicy.

For hundreds of years, food has been a Venetian obsession. As early as 1173, the doge of the day published a list of maximum permissible food prices. It was decreed in 1460 that no meal should cost more than a ducat a head. Later, a number of luxuries such as peacocks were banned and so was the practice, imported from India, of serving food wrapped in gold foil. But such sanctions were largely ignored. There are many contemporary descriptions and paintings of sumptuous Venetian banquets at which exotic foods, eaten with golden forks, were washed down by wine from exquisite Venetian glassware to the evident enjoyment of the lavishly dressed guests.

Corn was another Venetian introduction. It is the basis of *polenta*, which is served with almost everything and can be boiled, fried, broiled, or baked. It can be eaten instead of bread, with butter and cheese. And it is the inevitable accompaniment to *baccalà* (dried salt cod) and *uccelletti* (small roast birds, such as larks, robins, and thrushes, which the Venetians consume in great quantities).

Rice is another familiar adjunct to the Venetian meal, and the varieties of *risotto* are almost endless, featuring meat, vegetables, and, in particular, fish. One of the most delicious, *risi e bisi*, contains ham and peas.

84

In spite of its name, *risotto in capro romano* is typically Venetian and features mutton and tomatoes.

Polenta and rice are widely used but not to the exclusion of a rich variety of pasta dishes. *Fegato alla veneziana* (liver and onions) is, surprisingly, one of the few dishes to which Venice has given its name. In fact, the Venetians claim to have invented it.

Fish and shellfish, many of them unknown in other countries, are available in profusion and include soft-shelled baby crabs which are fried and eaten whole, *scampi* (shrimp), and *pescatrice* (angler fish), of which only the tails are eaten. Along more familiar lines are found such excellent seafood specialities as oysters and caviar, sole with herb sauce, roasted sardines with lemon juice, and a number of superb eel dishes. Other local specialities include *sfogi in saòr* (chilled sole with white raisins in wine sauce) and *insalata di seppioline e fagioli bianchi* (cuttlefish and navy bean salad).

Some other regional specialties and raw materials come from the neighboring cities of Padua and Rovigo. They include omelets, beefsteak with mushrooms in wine, a wide variety of coffees, sugar beets, and turkey. And from Verona, the city of Romeo and Juliet, comes *pandoro*, a vanilla-flavored cake that is perhaps the most popular cake in the region, and *mirtillo*, a very small red berry tart based on a fruit that resembles the cranberry. The city of Treviso contains some of the finest markets and foods in all Italy, offering delicious orange mushrooms, and a wide variety of fish, fruits, and vegetables. A truly indigenous Treviso vegetable is *radicchio*, a lettucelike plant that is not only delicious to eat, but magnificent to look at with its rose or pink coloring. The food of Trieste has a strong Hungarian influence. Typical of this is a dish which mixes gorgonzola cheese and mascarpone cheese with anchovy, caraway seeds, leeks, and mustard.

A rich and satisfying soup is *pasta e fagioli*, made of beans, onions, bacon, and tomatoes, sprinkled with grated cheese just before serving (or by each diner individually). Another is *zuppa di trippa:* soup with tripe, potatoes, and tomatoes, flavored with bacon, onion, and celery. *Pollo alla padovana* is a chicken rubbed with spices and roasted on a spit.

Most of these dishes characteristically use spices and herbs, notably nutmeg, saffron, and mint. Sugar is used to caramelize every kind of fruit and such dishes as *aranci caramellizzati* (caramel oranges with saffron-flavored *polenta*) are always available in Venetian restaurants.

Among local wines, Soave is outstanding. Many experts would grade it as the best of all Italian white table wines. The red Valpolicella is variable in quality but is always light and lively. Something of a rarity, the dry sparkling white Bianchetto Frizzante can be confidently recommended. These are among several regional wines that are becoming justly renowned throughout Italy. Bardolino is a light red table wine, drunk when between one and three years old.

Stewed Goose

RAGÙ DI OCA CON LUGÀNEGA

Serves 6

1 6-lb. goose
½ cup goose fat
1 large onion, peeled and sliced
   (about 1 cup)
1 large carrot, scraped and sliced
⅓ cup dry red wine
2 tbs. all-purpose flour
vegetable stock
1 clove garlic, peeled and crushed
⅔ cup tomato sauce (see page 43)
pinch of mixed spice (cinnamon,
   nutmeg, and allspice)
4 slices Canadian bacon
1 lb. _lugànega_ sausage

This dish is traditionally prepared with the homemade pure pork sausage, lugànega, _from Treviso. Commercially produced sausage may be substituted._

Cut the goose into pieces and season with salt and pepper. Heat half the goose fat in a casserole. Add the goose, onion, and carrot and sauté until browned. Add the wine and reduce it over moderate heat until evaporated almost completely; then sprinkle in the flour, a little at a time. Cook until golden brown, stirring constantly. Pour in enough stock to cover the goose completely; then add the garlic, tomato sauce, and mixed spice. Bring to a boil, cover tightly, and simmer for 1½ hours, or until the goose is tender.

Meanwhile, dice the bacon and cut the sausage into 2-inch pieces. Heat the remaining goose fat in a saucepan, add the bacon and sausage, and sauté for 5 to 10 minutes.

Drain the goose, place in a clean saucepan, and add the sautéed bacon and sausage. Strain the sauce over the goose through a fine sieve, place over low heat, and bring to a boil. Lower the heat, cover the pan tightly, and simmer for an additional hour. Serve very hot.

❧

Creamed Salt Cod

BACCALÀ MANTECATO

Serves 6

1¼ lbs. dried salt cod
3 cloves garlic
2½–3¾ cups milk
¼ cup olive oil
pinch of cinnamon

> Always soak dried salt cod in an enamel or earthenware pot, never in a steel, aluminum, or other uncoated metal container.

Frequently served on Friday, this dish is often accompanied by polenta.

Soak the fish for 24 hours in plenty of cold water, changing the water frequently. Drain, rinse under cold running water, and dry with a cloth or paper towels. Remove and discard any skin and bones and thinly slice the fish. Peel the garlic and rub over the inside of a ovenproof casserole or a large saucepan.

Place the fish in the casserole and add enough of the milk to cover it. Place the casserole over moderate heat and simmer until the mixture begins to darken in color. While the fish cooks, break it into small pieces with a wooden spoon. Heat the remaining milk and gradually stir into the casserole along with the olive oil to obtain a soft puree. It may not be necessary to add all the milk. Season with the cinnamon and salt and pepper to taste. Serve hot.

Braised Beef

MANZO ALLE ERBE CIÂR
IN PADIELE

Serves 6

2 lbs. rolled rump of beef
¼ lb. bacon fat
3 tbs. olive oil
1 small onion, peeled and chopped
1 small carrot, scraped and
    chopped
1 celery stalk, chopped
1 tb. minced parsley
¼ lb. ham fat
1 clove
6 coarsely cracked peppercorns
3 tbs. grated fresh horseradish root
pinch of oregano
vegetable stock or hot water
2 cups tomato juice
polenta (see page 25)

The strong flavor of the horseradish gives this casserole an unusual and delicious flavor. It is excellent served with hot polenta.

Preheat the oven to 350.

Make incisions all over the beef. Cut the bacon fat into strips and sprinkle with salt and pepper. Press the strips into the incisions in the beef. Heat the olive oil in a oven-proof casserole, add the onion, carrot, celery, parsley, and ham fat; sauté until lightly browned. Add the beef and sauté on all sides over high heat until browned. Add the clove, peppercorns, horseradish, and oregano. Remove from the heat and braise in the preheated oven for 1 to 1¼ hours, adding 1 tablespoon of stock occasionally to prevent the vegetables from sticking.

Remove the casserole from the oven, mix in the tomato juice, place over moderate heat, and simmer until the juice has reduced to a thick sauce. Remove the beef and carve into slices. Overlap the slices on an oval heated serving plate. Strain the sauce and pour over the beef. Serve immediately with hot *polenta*.

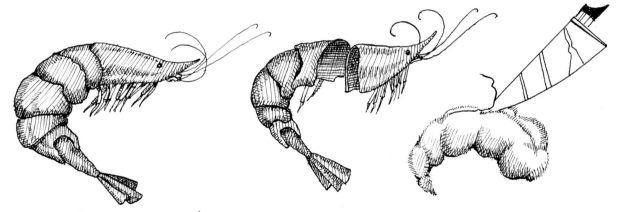

Fried Shrimp

SCAMPI FRITTI

Serves 6

24 fresh or frozen raw jumbo
    shrimp
all-purpose flour for coating
olive oil for deep-frying
3 lemons, halved

Many types of shellfish are popular in Venice and they are usually cooked only hours after having been caught. Scampi are very simply prepared in this dish, so their fine fresh flavor may be fully appreciated.

Peel the shrimp and dry well. Season with a little salt and coat with flour. Deep-fry a few shrimp at a time in hot oil for 3 to 4 minutes, or until cooked and crisp. Remove the shrimp, drain well on paper towels, and arrange on a round serving plate lined with a paper napkin. Sprinkle with salt. Garnish with the lemons and serve immediately.

In Veneto this dish is served on the night of the Feast of the Holy Redeemer, on the third Sunday in July. It must be prepared at least 24 hours in advance and may be served as an appetizer or an entree.

Rinse the fillets under cold running water and dry thoroughly with a cloth or paper towel. Coat each fillet with the flour. Heat about half the olive oil in a skillet over moderate heat, add the fillets, and sauté for 3 or 4 minutes on each side. Drain well and place on a cold serving dish. Pour the remaining olive oil into the skillet and add the onion, carrots, celery, bay leaves, and a little salt. Sauté the vegetables over high heat; then arrange them over the fish. Sprinkle with the white raisins and pignolias. Pour the wine and vinegar into the skillet and reduce by half. Pour it over the fish. Set aside to cool and keep in the refrigerator.

❧

Veal sweetbreads are the most commonly used in Italy. A whole sweetbread is the thymus gland, which is composed of two lobes. One lobe is rounder and more tender than the other; therefore it is more expensive if sold separately.

Preheat the oven to 400.

Cut each chicken liver in half. Season with salt and pepper. Heat half the butter in a skillet, add the livers, and sauté until firm but still soft in the center. Drain and cool. Cut the bacon into 24 pieces, each about ½ inch by 2 inches. Simmer the bacon in boiling water for 5 minutes. Drain and dry well on paper towels. Remove and discard any membrane from the sweetbreads. Cut the sweetbreads into 6 slices; then cut each slice into quarters. Cut the veal tenderloin into 24 pieces. Thread the liver, bacon, sweetbreads, and veal alternately onto 6 skewers, adding 1 sage leaf to each one. Season with salt and pepper and arrange on a baking sheet greased with the remaining butter. Place in the preheated oven for 15 to 20 minutes.

Meanwhile, sauté the *polenta* slices in the oil until golden brown and arrange on a serving plate. Place the skewers of meat on top and serve immediately.

Garnished Chilled Sole

SFOGI IN SAÒR

Serves 6

2 lbs. fillet of sole
all-purpose flour for coating
⅔ cup olive oil
1 medium onion, peeled and sliced (about ¾ cup)
2 small carrots, scraped and sliced
1 small celery heart, finely sliced
2 bay leaves
3 tbs. seedless white raisins
¼ cup pignolia nuts
1 cup dry white wine
1 cup vinegar

Skewered Meats with Polenta

POLENTA CON GLI OSELETI SCAMPAI

Serves 6

6 chicken livers
½ cup butter
1 lb. Canadian bacon
¼ lb. calf sweetbreads
1½ lbs. veal tenderloin
6 sage leaves
6 slices cold *polenta* (see page 25)
3 tbs. olive oil

Cuttlefish and Bean Salad

INSALATA DI SEPPIOLINE
E FAGIOLI BIANCHI

Serves 6

2 cups navy beans
2½ lb. cuttlefish or squid
1 large onion, peeled
1 large carrot, scraped
1 celery stalk
4¼ cups water

FOR THE DRESSING:
⅓ cup olive oil
¼ cup lemon juice
3–4 tablespoons cuttlefish stock
6 hard-boiled eggs, quartered

Squid is abundant in the waters around Italy and is served in a variety of ways. It is available in America, fresh or canned. This is an unusual fish salad, which may be served as a first course or as a main course or light luncheon.

Soak the beans overnight in plenty of cold water. Drain before using. Clean the cuttlefish, rinse under cold running water, and slice quite thickly. Cook the beans in plenty of lightly salted boiling water for about 45 or 50 minutes, or until tender. Drain well and set aside.

Place the onion, carrot, and celery in a large saucepan with water, salt, and pepper. Bring to a boil over moderate heat. Lower the heat and simmer for 5 minutes. Add the cuttlefish and simmer for about 1 hour, or until the fish is tender. Drain and set aside to cool. Discard the vegetables but reserve the required amount of stock for the dressing.

To make the dressing mix together the olive oil, lemon juice, and cuttlefish stock. Season with salt to taste. Place the beans and cuttlefish in a salad bowl and pour over the dressing. Garnish with the eggs. Mix together at the table before serving.

Beef Bouillon with Dumplings

KNÖDEL ALLA TIROLESE
IN BRODO

Serves 6

2 eggs
2 cups milk
½ cup butter
¼ onion, peeled and chopped
1 tb. minced parsley
½ cup finely chopped bacon fat
1 lb. stale white bread, cubed
¾ cup all-purpose flour
9 cups beef bouillon

The tiny dumplings are cooked in plain boiling water before being strained and added to the bouillon, so as not to cloud the pleasing clearness of the bouillon.

Beat together the eggs and milk. Heat the butter in a skillet over moderate heat, add the onion and parsley, and sauté until lightly browned. Add the bacon fat and heat gently for 2 to 3 minutes. Add the bread and sauté until lightly browned. Remove the skillet from the heat, transfer the contents to a bowl, and set aside to cool. Blend the flour and the egg mixture to form a firm paste. Set aside for 15 minutes.

Form the paste into balls, about the size of walnuts. Drop into lightly salted boiling water and simmer for 4 to 5 minutes, or until the dumplings rise to the surface. Remove the dumplings with a slotted spoon and drain well. Bring the bouillon to a boil and add the cooked, well-drained dumplings. Simmer for 2 to 3 minutes. Serve immediately.

Bass, a fish found in temperate waters, has been popular in Italy since the days of ancient Rome. Its flavor is particularly pleasing, and simple preparation allows it to be fully enjoyed. It is especially good when baked in the oven, as in this recipe.

Preheat the oven to 375.

Scale and clean the bass. Rinse under cold running water and dry with a cloth or paper towels. Make a diagonal slit on each side of the fish to help the heat to penetrate while cooking. Season with salt and pepper. Place the fish in a casserole with the butter and olive oil. Arrange the onion over the fish. Place in the preheated oven for 45 to 50 minutes, or until the flesh of the fish is firm and white. During cooking, baste occasionally with the juices in the casserole.

Carefully remove the fish from the casserole and place on a heated serving plate. Strain the juices left in the casserole and pour a little over the fish. Garnish the plate with the lemon slices and serve immediately.

Baked Sea Bass

SPIGOLA ARROSTO

Serves 6

1 3-lb. sea bass
¼ cup butter
1 tb. olive oil
1 medium onion, peeled and sliced (about ¾ cup)
2 lemons, sliced

Chicken Risotto

RISOTTO ALLA SBIRRAGLIA

Serves 6

1 chicken or chicken pieces, about
   2 lbs.
½ lb. lean stewing veal or beef
1 small carrot, scraped
1 small onion, peeled
2 celery stalks, chopped
½ cup butter
½ cup ground bacon fat
1 tb. chopped onion
1 tb. chopped carrot
⅔ cup dry white wine
3 large tomatoes (about ¾ lb.),
   peeled
2¼ cups plain uncooked rice
4¼ cups chicken stock
1 cup freshly grated parmesan
   cheese

Originally the chicken flesh for this dish was torn off the bones without the use of a knife. It was said to be so popular with the Austrian police during their occupation that it became known as "policemen's risotto."

Bone the chicken and reserve the bones and giblets. Cut the flesh into ½-inch cubes. Place the chicken bones, giblets, and veal in a saucepan with the carrot, onion, 1 chopped celery stalk, and a pinch of salt. Cover with water. Place over moderate heat and bring to a boil. Lower the heat and simmer gently for 30 to 40 minutes. Strain through a sieve and discard the chicken bones and the vegetables. Reserve 4½ cups of stock. The veal may be used in another dish.

Heat 1 tablespoon of the butter in a saucepan. Add the bacon fat, remaining celery, onion, and carrot, and sauté until lightly browned. Add the chicken, season with salt and pepper to taste, cover tightly, and cook for 3 to 4 minutes. Add the wine and reduce to 1 tablespoon. Add the tomatoes and simmer for 8 minutes. Add the rice and about 3 cups of the chicken stock. Simmer for 20 minutes, or until the rice is _al dente_, adding a little of the remaining stock as the rice absorbs the liquid. Remove the saucepan from the heat and stir in the remaining butter and 3 tablespoons of the cheese. Let stand for 1 to 2 minutes; then turn onto a heated serving plate and serve with the remaining cheese.

Poultry and game are popular in Italy and, throughout the ages, cooks have devised unusual ways of preparing duck, turkey, chicken, and goose.

Wash and dry the duck and cut into 4 portions. Set aside.

To make the marinade, place the onion, herbs, wine, salt, and pepper in a shallow glass or enamel bowl. Place the duck in the marinade and marinate for 48 hours, stirring occasionally.

Remove the duck from the marinade, drain well, and season with salt and pepper. Heat the olive oil and the butter in a deep skillet over high heat. Add the duck and sauté until well browned. Add the marinade and reduce by half. Blend the flour with a little of the water, then stir into the marinade. Lower the heat and simmer for 2 to 3 minutes, stirring constantly. Add the remaining water and the tomato sauce. Simmer over low heat for about 30 minutes, stirring frequently.

Meanwhile, peel the turnips, rinse under cold water, and slice thickly. Cook in lightly salted boiling water for 3 minutes. Drain the turnips and reserve the water. Heat the butter in a skillet, add the onion, and sauté until lightly browned. Add the flour with about ½ cup of the turnip water and mix thoroughly. Add the turnips. Simmer for about 30 minutes over moderate heat.

Remove the duck from the saucepan. Drain and place in a bowl. Strain the sauce through a fine sieve. Replace the duck and the strained sauce in the skillet and simmer together for 2 to 3 minutes over moderate heat. Place the duck in a heated serving dish and pour the sauce over. Serve immediately with the turnips.

Marinades are used to achieve several different results. Basically, foods are placed in a liquid so they will absorb flavor, give off flavor, or become more tender. Marination is hastened by higher temperatures, but so is the danger of bacterial activity. Therefore you should refrigerate any foods in their marinade if the marination period exceeds a couple of hours. Also, because of the acid quality of the wine marinade, you should soak the duck in a glass, earthenware, or enamel bowl—not a metal one—and use a wooden spoon for stirring.

Braised Duck with Turnips

ANITRA BRASATA CON RAPE

Serves 4

1 duck, about 4 lb.

FOR THE MARINADE:
1 small onion, peeled and chopped (about ½ cup)
1 tb. fresh chopped, or ½ tsp. dried, thyme
1 tb. fresh chopped, or ½ tsp. dried, rosemary
1¼ cups dry red wine

FOR COOKING THE DUCK:
1 tb. olive oil
3 tbs. butter
2 tbs. all-purpose flour
2 cups water
6 tbs. tomato sauce (see page 43)

FOR SERVING:
5–6 small white turnips
3 tbs. butter
1 tb. chopped onion
2 tbs. all-purpose flour

If you purchase fresh-killed duck, have it cleaned before you take it home. Check the skin for pinfeathers and pluck them out. Rinse the duck thoroughly in cold running water; scrub it inside and out with the exposed sides of a quartered lemon, then rinse again. To extract all the moisture from the inside, stuff the cavity with paper towels, repeating until the towels are dry when removed.

Venetian Beef Stew with Polenta

POLENTA PASTIZZADA
ALLA VENETO

Serves 6

2 cups *polenta* (see page 25)

FOR THE STEW:

1 lb. rolled rump of beef or rolled
    shoulder of veal

¼ cup olive oil

½ cup butter

1 medium onion, peeled and
    chopped (about ¾ cup)

1 medium carrot, scraped and
    chopped

2 celery stalks, chopped

1 tb. minced parsley

6 tbs. dry white wine

8 large tomatoes (2 lbs.)

2 cups dried mushrooms, soaked
    and drained, or ½ lb. fresh
    mushrooms, chopped

6 oz. chicken giblets, cleaned and
    sliced

1½ cups freshly grated parmesan
    cheese

Dried mushrooms should be soaked in warm water for a few minutes, drained, and then added to the dish. Look for cream-colored dried mushrooms; the black and gnarled ones often have a disagreeably strong flavor.

Cold polenta has been an alternative to bread for accompanying stews and meat dishes since the time of the Romans, when it was used as basic rations on the march. In this stew the cold polenta is combined with the meat to make a rich casserole.

Make the *polenta,* following the recipe on page 25. As soon as it is cooked and fairly soft pour onto a wet marble slab or wooden board. With a knife dipped in hot water, spread the *polenta* ¼ to ½ inch thick. Leave until cold.

To make the stew, cut the beef into ½-inch slices. Flatten them gently with a meat mallet or a wooden rolling pin and cut into 2-inch pieces. Heat half the olive oil and half the butter in a saucepan over moderate heat. Add the onion, carrot, celery, and parsley, and sauté for 2 to 3 minutes. Add the beef and sauté until golden brown. Season with salt and pepper. Pour in the wine and allow to reduce almost completely. Peel and press the tomatoes through a sieve to make a puree and add the puree. Bring to a boil, lower the heat, and simmer for 1 hour, or until tender.

Preheat the oven to 375.

Meanwhile, heat the remaining olive oil in a skillet, add the mushrooms, and sauté for 3 to 4 minutes. Drain well and add to the stew about 5 minutes before the end of the cooking time. Heat half the remaining butter in a skillet, add the giblets, and sauté until firm but still soft in the center. Set aside. Slice the *polenta* into long thin strips. Grease a deep baking pan or ovenproof casserole with half the remaining butter. Arrange a layer of *polenta* in the bottom. Spoon one third of the stew over the *polenta,* then one third of the giblets, and a sprinkling of the cheese. Arrange a second layer of *polenta* on top. Continue as above, ending with a layer of stew on top. Dot the surface with the remaining butter. Place in the preheated oven until the stew begins to bubble on the surface, which indicates that it is hot enough for serving. Serve immediately with the remaining parmesan cheese.

To peel a tomato, drop it into boiling water to cover for 10 seconds. Remove, cut out the stem, and peel. The blanching loosens the skin and it peels off easily. To seed and juice, cut the tomato in half crosswise and gently squeeze each half. If the juice is to be used, squeeze over a strainer placed on a bowl or measuring cup. For this recipe, place the peeled tomatoes in a sieve and press through with the back of a spoon.

In Italy, rice is often served as a salad. The different shell-fish give this recipe a typically Venetian flavor.

Scrub the clams and mussels and rinse well under cold running water. Place in a large saucepan with the wine. Cover tightly and place over high heat. Shake the saucepan gently until the shellfish open. Drain and set aside to cool. Remove the fish from their shells, discarding any that haven't opened. Shell the shrimp and simmer them with the scallops in lightly salted boiling water for 4 to 5 minutes. Drain well and dice them. Cook the rice in plenty of lightly salted boiling water for 15 to 20 minutes, or until *al dente.* Drain and set aside to cool.

Pound the eggs to a paste, using a pestle and mortar, or use a blender. Beating constantly, gradually add the oil. Add the saffron powder and Worcestershire sauce. Season with salt and pepper to taste. Mix the rice with the fish. Place in a glass bowl and cover with the sauce. Sprinkle with the parsley. Toss the salad at the table just before serving.

Rice and Shellfish Salad

INSALATA DI RISO
CON FRUTTI DI MARE

Serves 6

1 pint clams
1 pint mussels
¼ cup dry white wine
1 pint scallops
¼ lb. fresh or frozen raw jumbo shrimp
2¼ cups plain uncooked rice
3 hard-boiled eggs
about ¼ cup olive oil
pinch of saffron powder
few drops Worcestershire sauce
1 tb. minced parsley

Sicily and Sardinia

These are the largest islands in the Mediterranean, and they have a rich cuisine in common that displays the influence of successive waves of Phoenicians, Greeks, Carthaginians, Romans, Arabs, Normans, and Spaniards. Thus, on the same menu you will find *couscous*, a typically North African concoction of crushed grain and mutton or chicken, *cotogniata*, a sweet quince paste in the Greek or Turkish style, and traditional Italian pasta dishes. Great quantities are eaten in Sicily, particularly in the form of lasagne, colored green with spinach. *Pasta con le sarde* is a famous Sicilian dish with macaroni, sardines, pine-nut kernels, white raisins, saffron, and fennel. This should not be confused with the Sardinian *pasta de sarda*, in which the actual pasta flour is made of sardines, dried and crushed. In Sardinia superb homemade bread is a staple and is often substituted for pasta. However, one is not lacking for pasta dishes when in Sardinia. All the traditional favorites of the country can be found there along with some local specialties.

Sicily has no great indigenous meat dishes, whereas Sardinia has *càrrarglu*, suckling pig wrapped in herbs and aromatic leaves and buried under hot embers. Sardinia also raises goats and enormous flocks of sheep, both of which find their way into some of the island's most typical dishes. Wild boar, hare, partridge, and thrush are also popular.

Both islands have superb fish recipes. Tuna fish is served in a dozen ingenious ways, but the best is possibly the simplest: *ventresca*, thin slices of the fish's belly, brushed with olive oil and grilled. *Su ziminu* is the Sardinian fish soup. Excellent swordfish come from both islands, while Sicily can lay claim to superb mussels, prawns, squid, and gray mullet. Sardinia is best known for its sardine, lobster, eel, and trout.

There are many good vegetable dishes, and eggplants especially are stuffed and cooked in many different ways. *Caponata palermitana*, a splendid dish incorporating eggplants, ripe olives, celery, onion, tomatoes, and capers, originated in Sicily. Artichokes and other vegetables are made into tasty deep-fried fritters, called *fritelle*.

In Sardinia, pork appears in such varied forms as *bistecchine di cinghiale* (wild boar steaks), *carne a carrargiu* (boar—or calf, kid, or lamb—roasted outdoors), *favata* (pork sausage, stewed with beans and spices), and *porceddu* (spiced roasted suckling pig).

The Sicilians enjoy *arancina* (balls of minced meat, rice, egg, cheese, seasonings, and gravy, rolled in breadcrumbs and fried) and *anelletti gratinati* (cuttlefish dipped in a mixture of breadcrumbs, garlic and parsley, baked, and sliced into rings).

Oranges and lemons grow abundantly in Sicily and form the fruity basis of many ice creams, in the manufacture of which the islanders dispute pride of place with the Neapolitans. *Cassata* was invented in Sicily. A favorite Sicilian dessert is *cannoli alla siciliana*, Sicilian pastry horns filled with sweetened ricotta cheese mixed with pistachio nuts and candied peel.

As with the people of most other regions, Sardinians have their own special favorites when it comes to sweets. And many of them are associated with religious holidays. *Pabassinos*, made of egg dough, sweetened nuts and raisins, moistened with juice from green grapes, then shaped into cones and baked, are generally served at Christmastime; *angulis*, made from sweet dough and brightly colored decorations, is made especially for Easter.

Among Sicilian wines, the best known is Marsala, a rich brown sweet wine, which was created by an Englishman named Woodhouse as a rival to Madeira and became a favorite with Nelson's fleet in 1799. It is much used in the kitchen, for cooking kidneys and veal and, of course, in the preparation of *zabaglione*. Another Sicilian wine is Corvo, acrid and purple-black in color, like an eggplant. And there are appropriately fiery wines from the slopes of Etna.

Sardinia produces the unique white Vinaccia, which is dry, fragrant with almond blossom, and packs the kick of a mule. Many other Sardinian wines share, to a lesser degree, the impact of Vinaccia. The manner in which the vines are grown is important: closer to the ground than in most vineyards, and therefore absorbing more of the sun's heat, thus producing grapes which have a higher alcoholic content and a slightly coarse quality. The strength of these wines can be distinguished by their color. They range from a pink-tinged white to reds which are almost black. And the alcoholic content, while not quite rivalling Vinaccia, often reaches as high as 18 percent. It has been said that while the wines of Sardinia are not great, they most certainly are distinctive.

Cold Eggplant Appetizer

CAPONATA PALERMITANA

Serves 4

2 tender fleshy eggplants, about ½
   lb. each
½ tsp. salt
¼ cup cold water
6 celery stalks
¾ cup olive oil
1 large onion, peeled and thinly
   sliced (about 1 cup)
1 cup pitted ripe olives
4 large tomatoes (about 1 lb.),
   peeled and finely chopped
3 tbs. capers, drained
1 tb. pignolia nuts
⅔ cup white wine vinegar
2 tbs. sugar

Many claim that this dish was created in Sicily, though its origin is disputed. It is important to use a top-quality white wine vinegar to complement the delicate flavor of the eggplant and other vegetables.

Dice the unpeeled eggplants into ½-inch cubes and place in a bowl. Sprinkle with the salt and water. Set aside for 30 minutes; then drain well and rinse under cold running water. Squeeze lightly to remove the excess moisture, and dry thoroughly with a cloth or paper towels. Blanch the celery in boiling salted water, drain well, and dice.

Heat half the olive oil in a skillet over moderate heat, add the eggplants, season lightly with salt and pepper, and sauté until well browned. Remove the eggplants with a slotted spoon, drain, and set aside until required.

Pour any olive oil from the skillet and the remaining olive oil into a saucepan. Add the onion and cook over low heat until soft, but not browned. Add the eggplants, celery, and olives. Mix well; then stir in the tomatoes. Season with a pinch of salt and simmer for 10 to 15 minutes. Add the capers, pignolia nuts, vinegar, and sugar. Cover and simmer for an additional 15 minutes, or until the celery is tender, stirring frequently. Pour into a serving bowl and let stand until cold before serving.

> Most recipes for eggplant direct that it be macerated in salt before cooking. This is done, first, to eliminate a slightly bitter taste. Maceration is also important to remove excess vegetable water that otherwise exudes during cooking. Finally, salting prevents the blotterlike eggplant from absorbing too much oil or fat.

Green Sauce

SALSA VERDE

Makes 1 cup

1 large bunch parsley
2–3 anchovy fillets
3–4 pickled onions
1 small cold cooked potato
1 clove garlic, peeled and chopped
1 tb. chopped onion
6 tbs. olive oil
1 tb. vinegar

Sardinian green sauce is more pungent than the other green sauces found in Italy. It is often served with cold fish and is equally good with a variety of cooked vegetables, hot or cold meat, and as a dressing for an antipasto plate.

Place the parsley leaves in a mortar or mixing bowl with the anchovy fillets, pickled onions, potato, garlic, onion, and a pinch of salt. Pound the ingredients with a pestle or wooden rolling pin to form a soft paste. Place the mixture in a bowl and gradually add the oil, drop by drop, beating well after each addition until it resembles thick mayonnaise. Stir in the vinegar.

Macaroni with Sardines and Fennel

PASTA CON LE SARDE

Serves 6

¼ lb. anchovy fillets
⅔ cup milk
1 lb. fresh sardines
1 head fennel, about ¾ lb.
⅓ cup olive oil
3 cloves garlic, peeled
⅓ cup water
pinch of saffron powder
1 tb. minced parsley
4 tbs. chopped onion
¼ cup seedless white raisins
⅓ cup pignolia nuts
1¾ lbs. macaroni

Thomas Jefferson introduced macaroni into America. Along with French home furnishings, Tuscan wine, Lombardy poplars, and countless gourmet recipes gathered when he was Ambassador to France, Jefferson imported the first spaghetti-making machine into America.

Although Naples is now the main producer of pasta, it was first made in Sicily. Records dating back to 1250 mention it by its original name of maccaruni.

Soak the anchovy fillets in the milk for 10 to 15 minutes to remove the excess salt; then drain. Remove and discard the heads and tails of the sardines, clean them, and remove the backbones. Rinse thoroughly under cold running water and dry well with a cloth or paper towels.

Trim and wash the fennel and cut into 8 pieces. Heat half the olive oil in a saucepan over moderate heat and add 2 cloves of the garlic, the water, saffron, and 1 piece of fennel. Season with salt and pepper. Sauté together until golden brown; then add the sardines and cook for 2 to 3 minutes. Remove the saucepan from the heat and set aside. Discard the garlic. Place the remaining fennel in a second saucepan with boiling salted water to cover, simmer for 15 minutes, drain, chop, and set aside. Reserve the cooking water

Pound the anchovies to a paste with the parsley. Place the remaining olive oil in a skillet over moderate heat, add the remaining clove of garlic with the onion, and sauté until brown. Add the fennel, the anchovy mixture diluted with ½ cup of the cooking water from the fennel, the white raisins, and the pignolia nuts. Simmer over moderate heat for 2 to 3 minutes.

Preheat the oven to 350.

Place the remaining cooking water from the fennel in a third saucepan and bring to a boil. Add the macaroni and enough lightly salted boiling water to cover the macaroni. Simmer until the macaroni is *al dente*. Drain well and place the macaroni in layers in a heated casserole, alternating with layers of the sardine mixture and the anchovy mixture, beginning and ending with a layer of macaroni. Place in the preheated oven and bake for 20 minutes. Serve hot.

To cook pasta properly, it is essential to have a very big pot with rapidly boiling salted water. Unless the pasta cooks in sufficient water it cannot expand properly and shed its excess starch. One pound of pasta should cook in 6 quarts of rapidly boiling water to which 2 tablespoons of salt have been added. Pasta cannot be cooked in advance and, according to Italians, cannot be reheated.

The meticulous and painstaking Sicilian cooks take great pride in preparing this specialty of their region—rolled beef with egg and cheese stuffing.

Place the beef on a chopping board and beat it with a meat mallet or a wooden rolling pin to ½-inch thick. Season with salt and pepper and set aside until required.

To make the stuffing, slice the eggs and cheese and mix with the ham. Add the garlic, parsley, and oregano to the egg mixture. Season with salt and pepper. Spread the stuffing over the beef and roll up tightly to enclose the stuffing completely. Secure with fine string and season with salt and pepper.

Preheat the oven to 375.

Brush the beef thoroughly with olive oil and place in a well-greased ovenproof casserole. Place the onion, carrot, garlic, and bay leaf around the beef. Add the stock and bake in the preheated oven for about 1 hour, basting occasionally.

When cooked, remove the string, slice the *farsumagru*, and place on a heated serving plate. Add the wine to the remaining juices, reduce by half in a saucepan over high heat, and strain. Pour over the meat. Serve immediately.

Braised Stuffed Beef

FARSUMAGRU

Serves 6

2 lbs. round steak in 1 large slice

FOR THE STUFFING:
4 hard-boiled eggs
6 oz. soft caciotta cheese
¼ lb. ground ham, lean bacon, or
    sausage meat
1 clove garlic, peeled and chopped
1 tb. minced parsley
pinch of oregano

FOR COOKING THE FARSUMAGRU:
1 tb. olive oil
1 small onion, peeled and chopped
1 medium carrot, peeled and sliced
2 cloves garlic, peeled and sliced
1 bay leaf
4–5 tbs. beef stock or water
6 tbs. dry red wine

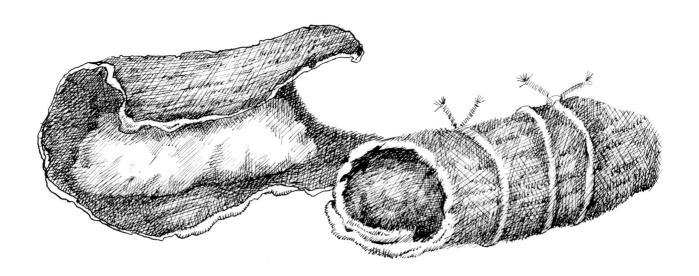

Kid Casserole

GRASSETO DI CAPRETTO

Serves 6

2 lbs. lean kid, veal, or lamb
6 tbs. olive oil
3 tbs. finely chopped onion
few sprigs parsley, tied together
2 oz. pecorino or other hard
   cheese, diced
4 cloves garlic
6 tbs. dry red wine
2 large potatoes, peeled and diced
   (about 2 cups)

Tender veal, or even young lamb, may be substituted if kid is not available.

Cut the kid into 1½-inch cubes. Season with salt. Heat the olive oil in a saucepan over moderate heat, add the onion, and sauté until browned. Add the kid, parsley, cheese, and unpeeled garlic and sauté until well browned, stirring frequently. Add the wine and reduce it to 3 tablespoons, stirring constantly.

Add the potatoes. Barely cover the kid and potatoes with warm water and season with a little additional salt. Bring to a boil, lower the heat, and simmer for 45 minutes, or until the kid is tender. Remove and discard the parsley and garlic and season the kid and sauce generously with pepper. Serve very hot.

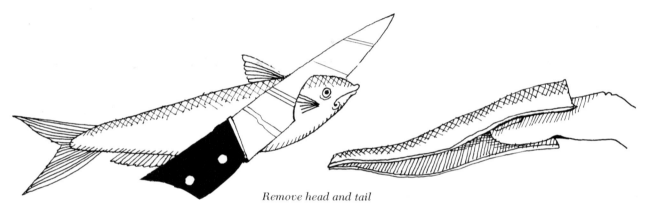

Remove head and tail

Stuffed Sardines

SARDE IMBOTTITE

Serves 6

24 large fresh sardines
1 clove garlic, peeled and chopped
⅓ cup pitted ripe olives, coarsely
   chopped
½ cup capers, chopped
½ cup minced parsley
½ cup fine fresh bread crumbs
olive oil

Sardines abound in the waters around the island of Sardinia, from whence they derived their name. They are used extensively in the cooking of the island, besides being salted and canned for export.

Remove and discard the heads and tails of the fish, clean them, and remove the backbones. Rinse thoroughly under cold running water and dry well with a cloth or paper towels. Place them skin-side down on a flat surface. Mix the garlic, olives, capers, parsley, bread crumbs, salt, and pepper together in a bowl. Add enough olive oil to bind the mixture.

Preheat the oven to 400.

Spread a little of the mixture on the flesh, fold the fish over the filling, and place in a greased casserole. Lightly sprinkle with olive oil, season with a little more salt, and cook in the preheated oven for about 20 minutes. Serve hot or cold.

Stewed Rabbit

CONIGLIO SELVATICO ALLA
CACCIATORA

Serves 6

2 lbs. rabbit pieces
all-purpose flour for coating
6 tbs. olive oil
1 tb. chopped onion
⅔ cup dry white wine
2½ cups beef stock or water
⅔ cup tomato sauce (see page
    43)
1 sprig parsley
1 bay leaf
1 cup button mushrooms

Many supermarkets carry an excellent quality frozen young
rabbit, cut up and ready for
cooking as soon as the pieces
are defrosted.

The rocky interior of Sardinia is rich in wildlife. Shepherds rely on game to provide them with food. This is a traditional recipe prepared by the shepherds' wives, who make it with wild rabbit.

Rinse the pieces of rabbit under cold running water, cut into 3-inch pieces, dry with a cloth or paper towels, and coat with flour. Heat 4 tablespoons of the olive oil in a skillet over moderate heat and add the rabbit. Season with plenty of salt and pepper. Lower the heat, add the onion, and sauté until lightly browned. Pour in the wine and reduce to 3 tablespoons. Add the stock and tomato sauce. Bring to a boil, stirring constantly. Tie the parsley and bay leaf together and add to the skillet. Cover tightly and simmer for 50 to 60 minutes, stirring occasionally.

Meanwhile, wipe the mushrooms with a damp paper towel. Heat the remaining olive oil in a skillet over moderate heat, add the mushrooms, season with a little salt, and sauté for 15 minutes. Add the mushrooms to the rabbit about 20 minutes before the end of the cooking time. Remove and discard the herbs. Serve immediately.

Baked Sardines

SARDE A BECCAFICU ALLA
CATANESE

Serves 6

24 large fresh sardines
3 cloves garlic, peeled and
    chopped
small bunch parsley, minced
½ cup grated parmesan cheese
all-purpose flour for coating
1 egg, beaten
fine bread crumbs for coating
1 tb. olive oil
3 lemons, halved

This is another Sicilian way of preparing sardines. The cheese is particularly delicious with the fish and gives it an unusual flavor.

Remove and discard the heads and tails of the fish, clean them, and remove the backbones. Rinse thoroughly under cold running water and dry well with a cloth or paper towels. Place them skinside down on a large plate. Mix the garlic, parsley, and cheese.

Preheat the oven to 400.

Fill the center of each fish with a little of the garlic mixture. Press together so the filling is completely enclosed. Coat the sardines in flour and dip into the egg and then into the bread crumbs. Grease a casserole with half the olive oil and place the sardines in it. Sprinkle with the remaining olive oil. Place in the preheated oven and cook for 30 minutes, or until the surface is well browned. Serve immediately from the casserole and garnish with the lemons.

Rice is not used as much in Sicily as in other parts of Italy, although it was introduced into Italy through Sicily by the Arabs. Here is this traditional island recipe for a rice snack.

Heat the olive oil in a skillet over moderate heat, add the onion, and sauté until lightly browned. Grind together the giblets, sweetbreads, and veal and add to the onion. Season with salt and pepper and simmer together for about 5 minutes. Pour in the wine and reduce it almost completely. Sprinkle in the flour and cook until browned. Add the stock and bring to a boil over moderate heat, stirring constantly until the sauce is well cooked and quite thick. Remove the saucepan from the heat and set aside to cool.

Cook the rice in plenty of boiling salted water for 18 to 20 minutes, or until *al dente*. Drain the rice and place on a table or a large tray, spreading with a wooden spoon to prevent it from sticking together. Let stand until cold. With wet hands, form the rice into balls, about 2 inches in diameter. Make a depression and fill with a little of the giblet mixture. Press the rice over the filling to seal it completely. Coat the balls in flour, then with the egg and bread crumbs. Place them, a few at a time, into hot oil. Drain when crisp and well browned. Serve immediately.

❧

Sardinia, the second-largest Mediterranean island, has known terrible periods of poverty and many people still eat very frugally. This soup results from the need to make a little go a long way.

Place the semolina flour and saffron on a wooden board or in a mixing bowl. Make a well in the center, pour in the water, and sprinkle the salt over the water. Bind together with the fingers to form a dough; then rub between the fingers till it crumbles into little pieces about the size of peppercorns.

Place the balls in a sieve and shake away the loose semolina flour, leaving the *fregula* in the sieve. Spread a cloth over a large plate, place the *fregula* on top, and set aside in the sun or in a warm place to dry. Bring the bouillon to a boil and add the *fregula*. Simmer until tender; then add the cheese and salt to taste. Serve very hot.

Sicilian Rice Croquettes

ARANCINE

Makes about 20 croquettes

6 tbs. olive oil
1 small onion, peeled and chopped
½ lb. each chicken giblets, lamb sweetbreads, and ground lean veal
6 tbs. dry white wine
2 tbs. all-purpose flour
⅓ cup vegetable stock or water
2¼ cups plain uncooked rice
all-purpose flour for coating
1 egg, beaten
bread crumbs for coating
oil for deep-frying

Semolina and Cheese Soup

FREGULA

Serves 6

2 cups coarse semolina
pinch of saffron powder
⅔ cup water
½ tsp. salt
9 cups beef bouillon
1 cup grated cacio cheese

Sicilian Pastry Horns

CANNOLI ALLA SICILIANA

Serves 6

FOR THE PASTRY:
3 cups all-purpose flour
¾ cup Marsala
pinch of sugar
olive oil for deep-frying

FOR THE FILLING:
¼ cup pistachio nuts
¼ cup mixed candied peel
1 lb. ricotta cheese
1 cup sugar

FOR THE DECORATION:
sifted confectioners sugar

These cheese-and-fruit-filled cones, which are a specialty of the Sicilians, are sold in pastry shops and in sidewalk restaurants throughout Italy. Their delicate and unusual flavor is from the Marsala wine that is used in the pastry. A steaming cup of espresso is often served with the cannoli.

Sift the flour and a pinch of salt onto a marble slab or into a mixing bowl and make a well in the center. Pour in the Marsala, add the sugar, and mix to a firm dough. Knead lightly until smooth, cover with a damp cloth, and set aside for about 2 hours.

Roll the pastry into sheets, about ½ inch thick, and cut into 4-inch squares. Roll each square around a cream-horn tin or a metal cone-shaped mold about 4 inches long, and set aside for about 30 minutes.

Heat the olive oil in a skillet and add the pastry-covered tins. Remove them when the pastry is golden brown and drain well. Place on a cloth to cool slightly. Slide the pastry horns carefully off the tins and let stand until cold.

To make the filling, finely chop the pistachio nuts and the candied peel. Blend thoroughly with the cheese and the sugar. Place the filling in a pastry bag with a large plain tip. Fill the pastry horns with the cheese filling and dust with confectioners' sugar.

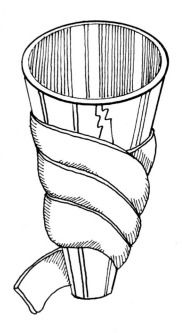

Roll pastry around mold

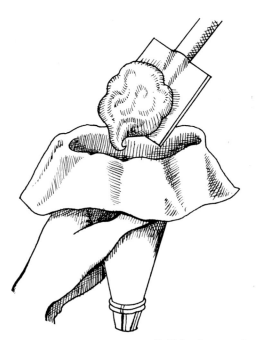

Fold back pastry bag and fill

Piedmont

Piedmont, in the extreme north, borders on France and Switzerland. It is a region of contrasts, ranging from the snow-capped Alps to the fertile rice paddies of the Po Valley, embracing heavy industry around Turin (the center of Italy's automobile, metallurgical, and chemical industries) and peaceful vineyards, orchards, and olive groves. Game abounds in the hills and dairy produce is plentiful. Because Piedmontese cooking relies heavily on butter and wine, it is often said to derive from France—however, it was the Romans who introduced the French to both products and Italian cooks who taught them their culinary uses.

What with the mountainous terrain, one might expect Piedmontese cooking to be of the hearty variety—and to a degree it is. However, the region also has a long-standing tradition of sophisticated cuisine, much of which was created in Turin, the capital of Piedmont. Thus, one may be surprised at the delightful subtlety of the food of the region.

Rice is the chief product, and in fact Piedmont is the largest rice-producing area in all Italy. The mountain streams provide carp and frogs. Frogs are a favorite ingredient in several regional dishes, the most popular of which is *rane dorate* (skinned frogs dipped in flour and fried in olive oil). Naturally, a host of dishes are prepared with rice. Of these, *riso al limone* (boiled rice with lemon) is one of the best.

The mountains of Piedmont offer some rather rare animals used in the preparation of unique dishes. There is wild goat, chamois, white hare, and wild boar, to name a few. As for more conventional meats, the average Piedmontese prefers mixed boiled meats to roasts. Such a typical regional specialty is *bolliti misti*—a mixture of beef, tongue, chicken, sausage, and veal cooked in a green sauce.

Or one could choose from *vitello tonnato* (veal with tuna fish sauce), *rognoni trifolati* (kidneys cooked in butter and wine), *stracotto di bue al barolo* (beef stew in red wine sauce). But we dare not overlook the Piedmontese pasta, of which they are particularly fond. Their favorite is *agnolotti*, small squares of dough similar to ravioli, made with egg and filled with meat, spinach, or cheese. As for soups, one of the most famous in the region is *busecca*, a thick broth of tripe and vegetables. Another excellent first course, more usually eaten as a snack, is *bagno calda*, the hot sauce of butter, olive oil, anchovies, and garlic, served with cold raw cardoons or white thistles, sliced cabbage, and cooked and raw pimentos.

In Turin the world-famous *grissini* (breadsticks) were created. Today you can find them in almost every Italian restaurant in the world. The region is equally famous for magnificent truffles.

There are some fine cheeses, including robiole (a spicy, creamy cheese) and the most famous of all, fontina, which with truffles forms the basis for *fonduta*, possibly the most famous of all Piedmont dishes (melted cheese, eggs, and usually grated truffles).

Generally speaking, mountain people include high-energy foods in their diet. This is certainly true of the Piedmontese, who enjoy highly sweetened desserts such as *dolce torinese* (a cold, rich chocolate loaf with almonds and butter cookies), excellent candied chestnuts, and *zabaglione*, perhaps the most renowned of Italian sweets, made from egg custard and sweet Marsala wine, beaten constantly over moderate heat until it is foamy and velvety.

One of the best-known Piedmontese wines is the white Asti Spumante, the sparkling, sweet white wine. The local red wines, which are among the finest in Italy, are widely used in Piedmontese cooking and are natural choices to accompany Piedmontese meals. Barolo, the best northern wine, deep reddish-brown in color, is strong and full of flavor. It should not be drunk until it is at least three years old. Its close cousin, Barbaresco, is another wine of quality, and should not be confused with Barbera, a coarse, rough *vin du pays*, drunk young, that ideally complements a garlic-laden dish like *bagno calda*. Grignolino is another good Piedmontese red wine. Vermouth, said to have been invented in Piedmont, is a very popular apéritif. Essentially it is white wine flavored with herbs, spices, roots, woods, etc. The exact formulas and proportions are the vermouth-maker's most essential property and are kept secret. In a vermouth company employing thousands of persons, there may be only two or three who know the formula—and in almost every case they are members of the owning family. Fifty million bottles of Italian vermouth are consumed yearly, and most of it is made in Piedmont. Much of that production no doubt finds its way into the most classic and probably the most favored of all cocktails, which has taken its name from one of the Turin vermouth companies—the Martini.

Stewed Beef

STRACOTTO DI BUE AL BAROLO

Serves 6

2½ lbs. beef rump roast
2 slices Canadian bacon
1 small carrot
1 celery stalk, chopped
1½ cups Barolo or other dry red
  wine
1 medium onion, peeled and
  chopped (about ¾ cup)
¼ lb. ham fat
2 cloves garlic, peeled and
  crushed
4 peppercorns
½ bay leaf
flour for coating
4 dried mushroom, soaked,
  drained, and chopped, or 4
  fresh mushrooms, chopped
¼ cup brandy

> When flaming food with warm
> brandy or liqueur, remember to
> avert your face as you ignite the
> liquid. Shake the pan gently so
> the flames spread evenly.

Some of Italy's best wines are produced in Piedmont, where Barolo has been famous for centuries. Barbaresco is a similar, somewhat less alcoholic, Piedmontese wine, but any rich, full-bodied red wine may be used in this recipe.

Wipe the beef with a clean damp cloth or paper towels. Cut the bacon into small strips. Scrape the carrot and cut into small strips. Using a sharp knife, make incisions all over the beef and insert the bacon and carrot strips.

Place the beef in a shallow glass bowl with the celery, the wine, and half the onion. Set aside to marinate for 8 hours, turning the meat occasionally.

Heat the ham fat in a large skillet over low heat. Add the remaining half onion, the garlic, peppercorns, and bay leaf and sauté until golden brown, stirring occasionally. Remove the beef from the marinade, dry well, and coat with the flour. Reserve the marinade. Brown the beef on all sides in the skillet. Lower the heat and add the mushrooms and the marinade. Season with salt and pepper and simmer over moderate heat for about 3 hours, or until tender, adding a little water occasionally as the sauce thickens.

Remove the beef from the skillet. Slice it and place on a heated serving plate. Strain the sauce through a fine sieve into a small saucepan and place over low heat. Heat the brandy gently in a second small saucepan; when reduced to 3 tablespoons, ignite and, while flaming, stir it into the sauce. Pour the hot sauce over the meat and serve.

Marsala Custard

ZABAGLIONE

Serves 4

4 egg yolks
½ cup sugar
1 tb. cold water
½ cup Marsala or other sweet
  white wine

This is one of the most famous of Italian desserts. Quick to prepare, it is an ideal emergency dessert.

In the top of a double boiler over simmering water, beat the egg yolks, sugar, and cold water. When the mixture is smooth and slightly thickened, gradually pour in the wine. Beat vigorously until thick and foamy. Remove the double boiler from the heat and beat a few moments longer. Pour into 4 large serving glasses and serve immediately. To serve cold, remove from the heat, place the top of the double boiler in a basin of ice chips, and beat until the custard is thoroughly chilled. Refrigerate until served.

Hot Garlic and Anchovy Dip

BAGNO CALDA

Serves 6

5 cloves garlic, peeled and finely
  chopped
1¼ cups milk
4 oz. anchovy fillets
1 cup olive oil
¼ cup butter
6 slices bread
raw vegetables, washed, trimmed,
  and chilled

It is important that the sauce be hot and the vegetables cold, as the contrast heightens the enjoyment of the dip. Several hours before you plan to serve the *bagno calda*, clean, trim, and slice the vegetables into chunks that the diner can pick up with his fingers. Then place the vegetables in a bowl of ice and refrigerate. Before serving, drain the vegetables.

In Piedmont, the cardoon—an edible thistle—is the favorite vegetable for dipping into this delicious hot sauce. If cardoons are unavailable, raw celery, fennel, bits of peppers, cauliflower, carrots, singly or in combination, are all excellent substitutes.

Soak the garlic in half the milk for 2 hours. Soak the anchovy fillets in the remaining milk for 10 to 15 minutes to remove the excess salt.

Drain the anchovy fillets and pound to form a paste. Heat the olive oil and butter in a small saucepan over very low heat, add the anchovy paste, and mix well. Add the drained garlic and continue cooking very gently for 20 minutes, stirring occasionally. The sauce must not boil or brown.

Pour the sauce into a chafing dish and place it over low heat in the middle of the table. Accompany it with the bread and the raw vegetables.

The green species is the olive from which oil is extracted—the black olive is used only for eating. The ripe olive is placed in a crusher which consists of a large circular vat, covered by a platform on which a heavy stone wheel revolves. A long horizontal bar is attached to the wheel, which crushes the olives and pits as it revolves. The pulp is then placed in large baskets and pressed.

White Sauce

BESCIAMELLA

Makes 2 1/2 cups

6 tbs. butter
2 tsps. finely chopped onion
¼ cup all purpose flour
2½ cups milk
pinch of nutmeg

This basic white sauce can be used on pasta, or for creaming such foods as vegetables and fish, or as a base for the preparation of other sauces.

Heat the butter in a saucepan over moderate heat. Add the onion and sauté until soft but not brown. Sift the flour over the butter and stir for 2 or 3 minutes to eliminate the uncooked flavor. Gradually add the milk, stirring constantly. Add the nutmeg and salt and pepper to taste. Bring the sauce to a boil, stirring constantly until it thickens; continue cooking over very low heat for 15 minutes. Use the sauce as required.

Gnocco *(the singular of* gnocchi*) means "dullard" or "puddinghead." But these delicious dumplings, particulary with the addition of the white truffle, found in the area, belie their uninteresting name.*

Scrub the potatoes under cold running water. Place them in a saucepan and cover with lightly salted cold water. Place the saucepan over moderate heat and bring to a boil. Lower the heat and simmer until barely tender. Drain and peel the potatoes; then press through a sieve onto a marble slab or into a mixing bowl. While still warm, make a well in the center and add the egg yolks and 2½ cups of the flour. Mix to a soft dough, adding a little more flour if necessary. Knead lightly until smooth. Divide the dough and, with floured hands, form into long rolls, about 1 inch in diameter. Cut the rolls into 1½-inch pieces and make a lengthwise groove on either side of each piece by pressing between the index and second fingers. Arrange them on a lightly floured surface, making sure they do not touch. Set aside for 10 to 15 minutes to dry.

Place a few *gnocchi* at a time into a large saucepan half filled with lightly salted boiling water. As they come to the surface, remove them with a perforated spoon, drain well, place on a large heated plate, and keep warm. While the *gnocchi* are cooking, heat the butter in a heavy saucepan until lightly browned. In another saucepan, heat the tomato sauce.

Cover the *gnocchi* with the cheese slices and sprinkle with the browned butter. Garnish with the truffles and serve immediately accompanied by the tomato sauce and grated parmesan cheese.

Potato Dumplings with Cheese

GNOCCHI FILANTI ALLA PIEMONTESE

Serves 6

8 large potatoes
2 egg yolks
about 3 cups all-purpose flour
½ cup butter
2 cups tomato sauce (see page 43)
6 oz. thinly sliced fontina or Swiss cheese
2 Alba truffles (optional), thinly sliced
1 cup freshly grated parmesan cheese

Fontina is a sweet and delicate semisoft cheese which comes from the Valle d'Aosta. It is made with infinite care but the finishing touch comes from its aging in well-aired stone buildings 10,000 feet above sea level.

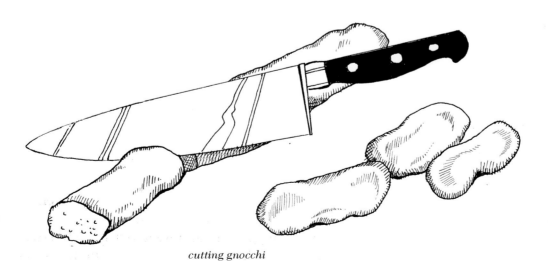

cutting gnocchi

Chicken Bouillon with Poached Eggs

ZUPPA ALLA PAVESE

Serves 1

1 cup chicken bouillon, heated
1–2 eggs
1 slice bread
¼ cup butter
6 tbs. freshly grated parmesan
   cheese

> An alternative way of preparing
> this soup is to place an egg on
> top of a slice of bread in each
> soup plate. Then carefully pour
> the hot bouillon into the plates.
> In this method, the egg is eaten
> nearly raw.

Francis I, King of France, pursued by the Spaniards after losing the battle of Pavia, stopped at a cottage and asked for food. The cook was preparing minestrone, _and in an endeavor to enrich this classic vegetable soup to befit the illustrious visitor, she toasted and buttered slices of bread, topped them with eggs and parmesan cheese, and poured the boiling soup over the top. Today a simple chicken bouillon is usually served, instead of_ minestrone.

Preheat the oven to 375.

Pour the hot bouillon into an ovenproof dish. Carefully add the eggs, without breaking the yolks, and season with salt and pepper. Place the dish in the preheated oven for 5 to 10 minutes, or just long enough to set the eggs lightly. Meanwhile, spread the slice of bread with butter, sprinkle with a little of the cheese, and cut into quarters. Sauté it in the remaining butter until golden brown. Arrange the pieces of fried bread in the soup, but not on top of the eggs, and bring to the table. Serve with the remaining grated parmesan cheese.

Homemade Sausage

GRIVA DELLA LANGA

Serves 6

1 pork caul
¾ lb. beef round steak, or lamb cut
   from the leg
¾ lb. pork liver
10 dried juniper berries
¼ cup fine fresh bread crumbs
6 tbs. freshly grated parmesan
   cheese
pinch of nutmeg
2 eggs
¼ cup butter
¼ cup olive oil

In Italy, there are many unusual sausages, from the homemade type, as in this recipe, to the commercially produced salame.

Soak the pork caul in boiling water for 5 minutes; drain well. Grind the beef, liver, and juniper berries together and place in a mixing bowl with the bread crumbs, cheese, nutmeg, eggs, salt, and pepper. Mix to form a paste. Spread the pork caul on a flat surface, fold in half and place the filling in a strip along the center. Roll the caul together over the filling to form a long sausage. Secure tightly with fine string.

Heat the butter and olive oil in a saucepan over moderate heat and add the sausage. Cover the saucepan tightly and gently cook the sausage for 1 hour, turning it occasionally. Add a little water, when necessary, to prevent the sausage from sticking. Remove the saucepan from the heat, take out the sausage, and remove and discard the string. Cut the sausage into thick slices and serve immediately.

Truffle Fondue

FONDUTA CON TARTUFI

Serves 4

⅔ cup milk
10 oz. fontina or Swiss cheese,
    thinly sliced
3 egg yolks
2 tbs. butter
4 slices toast
1 large Alba truffle, thinly sliced

> *Fonduta* differs from *fondue* in that it contains no alcohol and is never allowed to boil. It has the consistency of thick cream and is sometimes served over slabs of *polenta*.

Tartufi, the highly prized Piedmontese truffles, are edible fungi of an unusual and rare whiteness and are found in the Langhe area of Piedmont, south of Alba. Since no part of the truffle appears above the ground, dogs are taught to sniff them out. The truffle hunter then pries the truffle out with a curved iron tool.

Place 4 small ovenproof dishes in the oven to warm. Pour half the milk into the top of a double boiler over hot, not boiling, water and add the cheese and a pinch of salt. Stir vigorously until the cheese begins to melt and absorb the milk. Continue heating and stirring until the cheese has completely melted and the mixture is soft and creamy. Remove the double boiler from the heat immediately, since prolonged heating makes the cheese stringy.

Meanwhile, heat the remaining milk in a small saucepan until warm, remove from the heat, add the egg yolks, and stir until blended. Gradually add the egg mixture to the melted cheese, mixing thoroughly. Add the butter and beat until the mixture is smooth and glossy. Trim the crusts from the toast and cut each slice into 4 triangles. Arrange in heated ramekin dishes and pour the *fonduta* over the toast. Garnish with the truffle and serve immediately.

Braised Beef

CARBONATA

Serves 6

2½ lbs. boneless chuck roast
½ cup lard
5 medium onions, peeled and
    sliced (3½–4 cups)
2½ cups dry red wine
⅔ cup meat sauce (see page 64)
2 cups *polenta* (see page 25)

With this stew polenta *is served hot like mashed potatoes.*

Cut the beef into slices, about ½ inch thick, and flatten these lightly with a meat mallet or a rolling pin. Sprinkle with salt and pepper. Heat the lard in a skillet over moderate heat and sauté the beef on each side until lightly browned. Remove from the skillet and drain on paper towels. Place the onions in a saucepan. Cover with water and simmer for 5 minutes. Remove the onions from the saucepan with a slotted spoon and drain well on paper towels. Sauté the onions in the lard remaining in the skillet until lightly browned. Add a pinch of salt.

Preheat the oven to 400.

Lightly grease a 2-quart ovenproof dish and spread half the onions over the bottom. Place the beef on top and cover with the remaining onions. Add the wine and the meat sauce. Place in the preheated oven and cook for 2½ hours, or until the beef is tender and the liquid has evaporated. Serve with the *polenta*, steaming hot.

Unlike most game birds, quail should not be hung and is at its best within 24 hours of being killed. It has a delicious white flesh with a strong gamey flavor.

Preheat the oven to 400.

Pluck and clean the quail. Remove and discard the feet. Truss each quail with string to maintain its shape when cooking. Season the birds with salt and pepper and wrap each in a vine leaf and a slice of salt pork. Tie these securely with thread so the quail remains covered during cooking. Heat the butter in a skillet over high heat. Sauté the quail for about 20 minutes, or until golden brown all over. Transfer the quail to a roasting pan and place in the preheated oven for 10 minutes.

Meanwhile, prepare the *risotto*. Heat the butter in a saucepan over moderate heat, add the onion, and sauté until soft but not brown. Add the rice and salt and sauté for 2 to 3 minutes, stirring constantly. Add the stock, bring to a boil, and simmer for 20 minutes, stirring occasionally and adding a little more hot stock if necessary. Remove the saucepan from the heat when the rice is *al dente*. Stir in the cheese and set aside in a warm place for a few minutes.

Remove the quail from the oven and discard the thread, string, and salt pork. Place the *risotto* on a heated serving dish and arrange the quail on top. Heat the meat sauce and pour over the quail. Garnish with the truffle and serve immediately.

Quail with Risotto

QUAGLIE CON RISOTTO

Serves 6

12 quail
12 vine leaves
12 slices salt pork or fat bacon for barding
6 tbs. butter

FOR THE RISOTTO:
6 tbs. butter
1 tb. finely chopped onion
1⅔ cups plain uncooked rice
1 tsp. salt
about 4¼ cups chicken stock
1 cup freshly grated parmesan cheese
6 tbs. meat sauce (see page 64)
1 large Alba truffle, thinly sliced (optional)

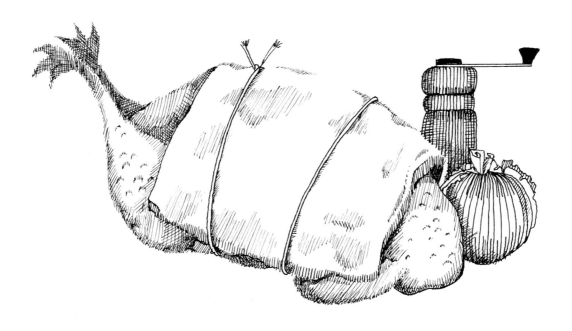

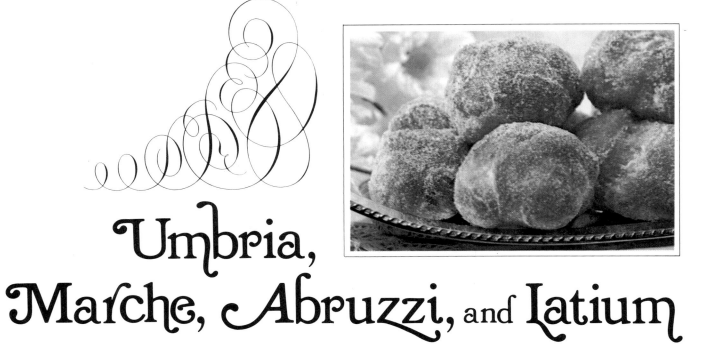

Umbria, Marche, Abruzzi, and Latium

These are four small provinces, strung across the middle of Italy from the Adriatic in the east to Rome in the west. They are sparsely populated, except for Latium, which contains Rome. Although they are lumped together, each has its individual landscape, history, and cuisine.

Umbria, for example, with a total population of less than a million, contains mountains and fertile valleys; plains, lakes, and rivers; and the provinces of Perugia—center of Etruscan culture—and Assisi, where St. Francis fed the birds. Unlike St. Francis, the Umbrians of today feed on the birds: a local specialty is *palombacci allo spiedo* (spit-roasted doves). This is a typically Perugian dish, as is *porchetta alla perugina* (roast suckling pig). Umbria is particularly noted for its ham, sausages, truffles, vegetables (celery, onions, mushrooms, cardoons), freshwater fish (trout, perch, gray mullet, and eel), rich chocolate, and its *pinoccate*, macaroons made from pine-nut kernels.

Orvieto, Umbria's notable white wine, is not unlike a white Chianti. It is available in all gradations, from very dry to quite sweet. Like many good Italian wines, it travels poorly. Other good regional wines include Trasimeno and the strong red Torgiano.

Marche is a mountainous eastern offshoot of the Apennines, and contains the Renaissance city of Urbino, and Ancona, an Adriatic port founded by the Greeks 3,500 years ago. The coastal towns have elaborate varieties of *brodetto*, rice fish stew poured over a foundation of toast and crowned, quite literally, with bay laurel. *Calcioni* is a local variety of ravioli, but baked in the oven. *Pasticciata*, a *polenta*-based dish, is also treated in this way. The white wines of the Castelli di Iesi, produced from the verdicchio grape and often marketed under that name, are cheap, unpretentious, and agreeable—a typical *vin du pays.*

South of the Marche lies Abruzzi, hilly where it is not mountainous, and with an agricultural and pastoral economy. Wheat, potatoes, grapes, olives, mutton, and white vinegar are important products. The Adriatic provides fish for yet more varieties of *brodetto,* and there are such novelties as *polpo in purgatorio* (octopus cooked in oil and tomato) and *scapece* (fried fish pickled in vinegar and saffron). Among the pasta dishes for which the region is renowned are *pincisgrassi,* baked pasta alternated with layers of cheese and a bolognese-type sauce, and *macaroni alla chitarra,* with a sauce compounded of olive oil, garlic, and red peppers.

Among the region's grand variety of desserts is a rich chocolate cake called *parozzo.* Of the local wines, Montepulciano, a really excellent dry red, is paramount. There is an almost equally good dry white wine, Trebbiano. The aromatic mountain herbs provide the basis for various digestives. The best known is Centerbe, which means "one hundred herbs." It comes in two types, strong and mild; the strength refers to the herbs rather than the alcoholic content, which is high in both. The strong is brewed for its medicinal effect and its taste is bitter. The mild contains wormwood, the basis for absinthe. Another local product is Aurum, an orange-flavored liqueur.

Despite the overwhelming dominance of the Roman metropolis, peasant traditions of regional cuisine persist in the province of Latium. Thrifty but delicious meals of offal (entrails) and meat are a feature. Oxtails form the basis of *coda di bue alla vaccinara,* lamb's pluck and artichokes of *coratella di abbacchio con carciofi,* and brains, sweetbreads, and zucchini of *fritto scelto. Trippa alla romana* is a noble dish. Quantities of spaghetti and macaroni are eaten, usually with a sauce incorporating diced bacon.

Another specialty is *abbacchio,* a casserole of lamb and anchovies; so is *saltimbocca* (slices of veal and ham cooked in butter, wine, and sage). From the towns of Latina and Gaeta come excellent shrimp and lobster. There are many delicious green salads, and several good local cheeses, of which two, the soft, creamy ricotta and the hard, sharp pecorino, are made of ewes' milk. The wines of the Alban hills are pleasant enough but fall short of excellence. Frascati, the most famous of the Castelli Romani wines, and the decidedly sweet Est! Est!! Est!!! are the best-known of the whites, but Grottaferrata, full and mellow, is often thought better than either. As regards other liquor, there are the pleasant local anisettes, Mistra and Sambuca. A Roman custom is drink the sweet liqueur *con le mosche,* that is, "with flies." The fly is a coffee bean. It is dropped into the Sambuca and at the same time as the liquid is sipped, the bean is crunched. The sharp flavor of the coffee bean tempers the sweetness of the liqueur. As a change from wine, the local beer, Birra Peroni, is as good as any in Italy.

Grilled Lamb Chops

BRACIOLETTE DI ABBACCHIO
A SCOTTADITO

Serves 6

6 loin lamb chops, about 2–2½ lb.
2 tablespoons lard

The tasty and tender lamb from this region is best cooked simply and without embellishment. The name means "lamb chops to burn [your] fingers," for traditionally they were turned over with the fingers.

Trim any excess fat and skin from the chops and flatten with a meat mallet or a wooden rolling pin. Season with salt and pepper. Melt the lard and brush over the lamb. Grill the chops over a charcoal fire until well browned and tender. Alternatively, cook under a moderately hot broiler for about 15 minutes. Serve hot.

Anchovy Omelet

FRITTATA CON ACCIUGHE

Serves 6

6 anchovy fillets
¼ cup milk
1 tb. chopped parsley
¼ cup olive oil
1 clove garlic, peeled and chopped
3 tomatoes (about ¾ lb.), peeled and chopped
1 small chili pepper
10 eggs

The anchovies are an integral part of the omelet, which is cooked on both sides and served flat.

Soak the anchovies in the milk for about 10 minutes to remove the excess salt. Drain them and pound to a paste with the parsley. Heat one third of the olive oil in a skillet over moderate heat, add the garlic, and sauté until lightly browned. Discard the garlic and add the anchovy mixture to the skillet, then add the tomatoes and chili pepper, and season with a little salt. Continue cooking for 8 minutes. Discard the chili pepper, pour the mixture into a bowl, and let stand until cool.

Beat the eggs well and stir into the cooled anchovy mixture. Season with salt and pepper. Heat half the remaining oil in the skillet over moderate heat and pour in the egg mixture. Stir for a few seconds until the bottom of the omelet is golden brown. Continue cooking for a minute or two until the mixture begins to set. Remove the skillet from the heat and invert the omelet onto a large round plate. Heat the remaining oil in the skillet and slide the omelet into the skillet with the browned side up. Cook until golden brown; then slide the omelet onto a round heated serving plate and serve immediately.

> The root, stems, and leaves of parsley plants are high in protein. They are flavorful in themselves and are effective in blending the flavor of other herbs. Curly-leafed parsley is the type most commonly found in markets. Also available, and worth seeking, is the pungent flat-leafed Italian parsley.

> Italian omelets are not soft inside, as are French omelets. Well-cooked on both sides, Italian omelets are rather like flat cakes, resembling a pancake. They are served cut into flat wedges. Often, cooked leftover vegetables and/or meats are added to the egg mixture to cook with it. An onion or other raw vegetable can be quickly sautéed before the addition of the eggs.

Seafood Risotto

RISOTTO CON FRUTTI DI MARE

Serves 6

1 pint clams
1¼ pints mussels
¼ cup dry white wine
6 tbs. olive oil
1 medium onion, peeled, and
    chopped (about ¾ cup)
2¼ cups plain uncooked rice
4¼ cups boiling water
1 pint scallops, chopped
¼ lb. fresh or frozen raw jumbo
    shrimp, shelled, deveined, and
    chopped
1 tb. chopped parsley

It is important to use a mixture of varied shellfish to create a really authentic seafood risotto.

Wash the clams and mussels thoroughly under cold running water. Heat the wine in a saucepan over high heat. Add the clams and mussels and shake the saucepan over the heat until they open. Pour them into a colander with a bowl underneath to catch the cooking liquid. Remove the flesh from the shells and reserve. Strain the cooking liquid.

Heat the olive oil in a large saucepan over moderate heat, add the onion, and sauté until lightly browned. Add the strained cooking liquid, and reduce by half. Add the rice, pour in the boiling water, and stir. After about 10 minutes, mix in the scallops, clams, mussels, and shrimp. Season with salt and a little pepper. Continue cooking over high heat, occasionally adding 1 tablespoon of boiling water as the rice thickens and dries out. When the rice is *al dente* add the parsley and pour into a deep heated serving dish.

Sweetbreads in Marsala and Meat Sauce

ANIMELLE DI AGNELLO ALLA ROMANA

Serves 6

1 lb. lamb sweetbreads
1 lb. fresh mushrooms
½ cup butter
1 tb. finely chopped onion
6 tbs. Marsala
⅔ cup meat sauce (see page 64)

Sweetbreads should be bought the day they are to be cooked and then only if your butcher guarantees them to be absolutely fresh. They must be thoroughly cleaned before being cooked.

Lamb sweetbreads are considered a delicacy in Italy. They are often fried, sometimes with slices of ham, but in this recipe from Rome they are served in meat sauce, flavored with Sicilian Marsala.

Soak the sweetbreads in cold water for 30 minutes; then drain and rinse. Place them in a saucepan, cover with cold water, and bring to a boil over moderate heat. Boil for 1 minute; then drain and rinse again under cold running water. Remove and discard any skin and coarse tissue and dry the sweetbreads thoroughly with a cloth or paper towels. Wipe the mushrooms clean with a damp paper towel and slice thickly.

Heat 4 tablespoons of the butter in a skillet over moderate heat. Add the sweetbreads, onion, and salt and pepper and sauté until golden brown. Remove the contents of the skillet, drain, and keep hot. Add the mushrooms and a pinch of salt to the skillet, sauté until soft over moderate heat, remove, drain, and keep hot with the sweetbreads.

Pour the Marsala into the juices remaining in the skillet and reduce it by half over high heat. Stir in the meat sauce and simmer to reduce and thicken the sauce. Stir in the sweetbreads, onion, and mushrooms and add the remaining butter. Stir together for a few seconds before serving.

In Rome, where this dish is usually prepared with cardoons, it is also called stufatino al gobbo, *"stew with hunchbacks," since cardoons (gobbi) droop over at the top.*

Slice the beef and season with salt and pepper. Heat the lard in a heavy casserole or skillet over moderate heat, add the onion, celery, and bacon, sauté until browned. Add the beef slices and sauté on each side. Pour in the wine and reduce it by half. Add the tomato sauce. Continue cooking for 2 to 3 minutes; then add enough water to barely cover the beef. Cover the pan tightly and simmer over low heat for 2 hours, or until tender.

Add a few tablespoons hot water if the sauce thickens too much.

Meanwhile, separate the stalks of the celery, trim, wash under cold running water, and slice thinly. Cook the celery in boiling salted water until barely tender. Drain well. A few minutes before serving, mix the celery with the garlic and marjoram and stir into the beef. Serve hot.

Beef Stew with Celery

STUFATINO DI BUE CON SEDANI

Serves 6

2 lbs. arm pot-roast of beef
1 tb. lard
¼ onion, peeled and chopped
1 celery stalk, finely chopped
3 slices bacon, chopped
⅔ cup dry white wine
⅔ cup tomato sauce (see page 43)
1 bunch celery or cardoons
1 clove garlic, peeled and chopped
few sprigs marjoram, chopped

Fresh Peas with Ham

PISELLINI DOLCI AL PROSCIUTTO

Serves 6

6 tbs. olive oil or melted lard
½ small onion, peeled and chopped
3 lbs. fresh peas, shelled (about 3 cups)
4–6 tbs. vegetable stock or water
6 oz. prosciutto, sliced thinly into strips
fried croutons

Italians love fresh vegetables and have their own ideas about them. To be perfectly prepared, vegetables must not be overcooked, never watery, and must always be served in a heated dish immediately after cooking. The green peas that are grown around Rome are renowned for their sweetness. Cooked with ham, they are served as a vegetable dish or as a sauce for pasta.

Heat the olive oil in a skillet over moderate heat, add the onion, and sauté until lightly browned. Add the freshly shelled peas, season with a pinch of sugar, salt, and pepper, and pour in the stock. Simmer gently for 10 to 15 minutes. A few minutes before the peas are tender, add the ham. Discard any excess liquid. Serve in a heated vegetable dish, surrounded with freshly fried croutons.

To make croutons, dice fresh or dry bread into small cubes. Sauté the cubes in butter until they are lightly browned on all sides, adding more butter as necessary. Alternatively, you can butter slices of bread, cut them into dice, and brown in a 375° oven.

These tomatoes are excellent either hot or cold.

Rinse the tomatoes under cold running water and dry with a cloth or paper towels. Remove the top from each to form a lid. Remove the pulp from the inside of each tomato and press through a fine sieve. Reserve the pulp but discard the seeds remaining in the sieve. Strip the mint leaves from the stems and pound to a pulp along with the garlic. Place the rice in a bowl with the tomato pulp, garlic mixture, 2 tablespoons of olive oil, ¼ teaspoon salt, and pepper. Blend together thoroughly.

Preheat the oven to 425.

Place the tomatoes in a greased casserole and sprinkle with half the remaining olive oil and salt. Fill each tomato two-thirds full with the rice mixture; then cover with the lid. Mix the water into the tomato paste and pour into the casserole. It should reach halfway up the sides of the tomatoes. Sprinkle the tomatoes with the remaining oil and salt; place in the preheated oven. Cook for 40 minutes.

Stuffed Tomatoes

POMODORI COL RISO

Serves 6

12 firm medium tomatoes
small bunch mint
2 cloves garlic, peeled
¾ cup plain uncooked rice
¼ cup olive oil
½ tsp. salt
⅔ cup water
1 tb. tomato paste

Pot Roast

MANZO GAROFOLATO

Serves 6

2 lbs. rolled rump of beef
4 cloves garlic, peeled and
    chopped
1 tsp. chopped marjoram
¼ cup bacon fat
6 tbs. ground ham fat
1 tb. lard
1 medium onion, peeled and
    chopped (about ¾ cup)
1 medium carrot, scraped and
    chopped
4 celery stalks, chopped
2 tsps. minced parsley
pinch of nutmeg
2–3 cloves
⅔ cup dry red wine
5 large tomatoes (1½ lbs.), peeled

The wine most used by the Romans in their cooking and for the table is from the Castelli region. Today it is transported to Rome in trucks, but it used to be carried in horse-drawn carts which filled the roads at night. Most of the wine is used locally and little is exported.

Make incisions all over the piece of beef with a sharp knife. Mix 3 of the chopped garlic cloves with the marjoram. Cut the bacon fat into fine strips and roll in the garlic mixture. Season the strips with salt and pepper and press into the incisions in the beef.

Heat the ham fat and lard in a casserole over moderate heat. Add the onion, carrot, celery, the remaining garlic, and parsley. Tie the meat with fine string so it will maintain its shape during the cooking and place in the casserole. Sauté until browned; then add the nutmeg and cloves. Season with salt and pepper. Pour in the wine and reduce almost completely over high heat. Press the tomatoes through a sieve and add them along with enough water to barely cover the beef. Cover the casserole tightly and simmer over moderate heat for 2 hours, or until tender. Remove the beef from the saucepan, remove and discard the string, and carve into slices. Arrange on a heated serving plate and keep hot. Reduce the sauce until fairly thick and strain it over the meat. Serve very hot.

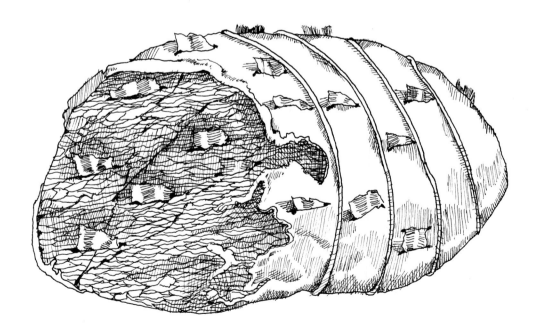

Ricotta, a particular favorite of the Romans, is often served with pasta in this way. You can substitute commercial egg noodles for the homemade ones.

To make the pasta, lightly beat together the eggs and olive oil in a small bowl. Sift the flour and salt onto a marble slab or into a mixing bowl and make a well in the center. Pour in the eggs and the oil, mix to a firm, smooth dough, and knead well. Wrap in a damp cloth and set aside for about 30 minutes.

Roll out the dough on a floured surface into sheets, about 8 inches wide, 12 inches long, and ¹⁄₁₆ inch thick. Fold each sheet in half lengthwise, then in half lengthwise again, several times. Cut the roll into ¼-inch ribbon noodles. Unfold the noodles, arrange them on a floured surface, and allow to dry for about 30 minutes. Place the noodles in a large saucepan half filled with lightly salted boiling water and simmer for about 8 minutes, or until *al dente.* Drain in a colander over a bowl and place on a heated serving plate. Reserve the cooking water.

Press the ricotta cheese through a sieve over the noodles and sprinkle with olive oil, salt and pepper, and, if necessary, a little of the water in which the noodles were cooked, to help melt and blend the cheese. Mix together and serve.

❧

The sage gives this dish its characteristic flavor. Directly translated, the name means "jump into the mouth," which the veal almost does when superbly cooked!

Flatten the veal with a meal mallet or a wooden rolling pin. Season with salt and pepper; then place 1 sage leaf and 1 slice ham on each piece of veal. Roll the veal or fold in half, and secure with a wooden toothpick. Coat lightly with flour.

Heat 3 tablespoons of the butter in a skillet over moderate heat and fry the veal until evenly browned and tender. Remove the toothpicks, place the veal on a heated serving plate, and keep hot.

Pour the wine into the skillet and reduce it to 1 tablespoon over high heat. Stir with a wooden spoon to loosen the residue on the bottom of the pan. Stir in the remaining butter, simmer for a few seconds, and pour the sauce over the *saltimbocca.* Serve immediately.

Noodles with Ricotta Cheese

FETTUCCINE FRESCHE
CON LA RICOTTA

Serves 6

FOR THE PASTA:
5 eggs
1 tb. olive oil
4 cups all-purpose flour
1 tsp. salt

FOR THE TOPPING:
¾ lb. ricotta cheese
4–5 tbs. olive oil

Veal with Ham and Sage

SALTIMBOCCA

Serves 6

12 veal scallops
12 fresh sage leaves
12 slices prosciutto
all-purpose flour for coating
½ cup butter
6 tbs. dry white wine

Spaghetti with Bacon, Egg, and Cheese

SPAGHETTI ALLA CARBONARA

Serves 6

1¼ lb. spaghetti
1 tb. olive oil
6 slices Canadian bacon, diced
6 eggs
½ cup freshly grated pecorino cheese
4–5 tablespoons light cream (optional)
¼ cup butter

The Sabine, a dairy district, is especially noted for its pecorino cheese, a firm sharp cheese which, grated, is used in cooking or at the table. For this dish, it is important to time the spaghetti so that it is cooked and drained just as the egg mixture begins to thicken.

Cook the spaghetti in plenty of salted boiling water for 10 to 12 minutes, or until *al dente*. Drain well. Heat the olive oil in a small skillet over moderate heat, add the bacon, and sauté until brown. Beat the eggs in a bowl; stir in the cheese, salt and pepper, and the cream, if used.

Melt the butter in a large saucepan and, when it is a nut-brown color, pour in the egg mixture, allowing it to thicken only slightly. Add the spaghetti and the bacon. Remove the saucepan from the heat, mix well, and serve.

It is always difficult to say exactly how much pasta to cook for a given number of people. It all depends. If the pasta dish is the meal itself, with a salad and dessert, then more pasta would be required than if it is the first of several courses. Pasta swells in cooking: 8 ounces of spaghetti will yield 5 cups cooked; 8 ounces of egg noodles, 4 cups cooked. Generally speaking, 1 pound of pasta will feed 4 to 6 people.

Spaghetti with Bacon and Cheese

SPAGHETTI ALLA GRICIA

Serves 6

1½ lbs. spaghetti
3 tbs. olive oil
2 tbs. lard
10 slices bacon, diced
¼ chili pepper
1 small onion, peeled and chopped (about ½ cup)
1 clove garlic, peeled and chopped
1 cup freshly grated pecorino cheese

Spaghetti is usually served in Italy as part of a meal. However, the addition of bacon and cheese makes this a meal in itself. It is frequently served at the tables of the roadside trattorias, *washed down, no doubt, with one of the local wines, the Castelli.*

Cook the spaghetti in plenty of salted boiling water for about 10 to 12 minutes, or until *al dente*. Drain, turn into a deep heated serving dish, and keep hot.

Heat the olive oil with the lard in a skillet over moderate heat and add the bacon and chili pepper. When the bacon begins to brown, remove it from the skillet and set aside. Add the onion, garlic, and a pinch of salt to the skillet, stir together, and remove from the heat when lightly colored. Discard the chili pepper and add the bacon. Sprinkle the spaghetti with the bacon mixture and the cheese. Mix at the table and serve immediately.

Braised Dried Cod

STOCCAFISSO A POTACCHIO

Serves 6

1¼ lb. dried cod or stockfish
¾ cup olive oil
1 medium onion, peeled and
    chopped (about ¾ cup)
few sprigs fresh or dried rosemary
¼ chili pepper
6 tbs. dry white wine
⅔ cup tomato sauce (see page 43)
⅔ cup water
¼ cup butter

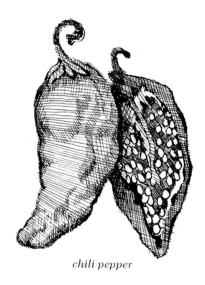

chili pepper

Dried fish, a Venetian favorite, is given a very rich treatment in this region. The wine, herbs, and pepper make it into a succulent fish stew.

Soak the fish overnight in plenty of cold water. Drain and pat dry with a cloth or paper towels. Remove and discard any skin and bones. Heat the oil in a large earthenware casserole, add the onion, and sauté with the rosemary until golden brown. Add the fish and the chili pepper and sauté for about 5 minutes, or until beginning to brown. Add the wine and simmer until reduced by half.

Remove and discard the rosemary and chili pepper. Add the tomato sauce blended with the water. Season lightly with salt and continue simmering for 1 hour.

Preheat the oven to 425.

Cut the butter into small pieces and place on top of the fish. Place in the preheated oven for 5 to 10 minutes, or until golden brown. Serve very hot.

> The volatile juices and oils contained in a chili pepper can burn your hands, fingers, and eyes. Wear rubber gloves, keep your hands away from your face, and work in a well-ventilated area while holding the chilis under cold running water. Never work under hot water, as the fumes can cause painful irritation to your eyes and nose. Cut out the stem, and if you wish to remove the seeds, the hottest part of the chili, slice it in half and brush them out with your finger. If the inside ribs are thick and fleshy, cut them out with a small, sharp knife.

Mixed Fried Fish

FRITTO MISTO DI MARE

Serves 6

6 lbs. of assorted fish: small sole,
    red mullet, or fresh sardines
⅓ cup olive oil
3 tbs. lemon juice

Freshly caught fish tastes even better when cooked outdoors, and this simple recipe is ideal for camp-style or picnic dining. The types of fish used can be as varied as you wish, and a mixture will produce an interesting flavor. A chilled Chianti or perhaps a light Italian beer will complete the meal.

Clean each fish and wash under cold running water. Heat the olive oil in a skillet over moderate heat. Add the fish, without drying or flouring them. When cooked, drain and sprinkle generously with salt and the lemon juice. Place on a large serving plate and serve immediately.

This rich dessert was bestowed by the Neapolitans on Lord Nelson after his victory in 1798 over Napoleon in Egypt. "English soup," as it is called, was the creation of an anonymous pastry cook, smitten with the Admiral and the English and their spirit-soaked trifles.

Cut the sponge cake into thin pieces and place them on two plates. Sprinkle the liqueur over the cake on one plate, and the rum, diluted with the water, over the remaining cake. Set aside for 20 to 30 minutes.

To make the custard, scald the milk in a small saucepan. Mix the sugar and flour together in a second saucepan. Lightly beat the egg yolks and blend into the sugar mixture. Gradually stir in the hot milk. Place over low heat and cook for about 5 minutes, or until the mixture thickens, stirring constantly with a wooden spoon or wire whisk. It should be a thick pouring consistency. Spread ¼ cup of the custard on a round ovenproof serving plate, about 12 inches in diameter. Arrange the cake soaked in liqueur on top. Add the candied peel to the remaining custard, stir, and spoon over the cake. Arrange the sponge slices soaked in rum on top in a dome shape.

Preheat the oven to 325.

To make the meringue, beat the egg whites until stiff and fold in the sugar. Spread the meringue smoothly over the surface of the trifle with a spatula. Decorate with the orange peel and lightly sprinkle with sugar. Place in the preheated oven for about 30 minutes, or until the meringue is lightly colored. Remove from the oven and set aside to cool before serving.

Trifle

ZUPPA INGLESE

Serves 6

1-lb. sponge cake
¼ cup Alchermes liqueur or fruit
   liqueur
¼ cup rum
1 tb. cold water

FOR THE CUSTARD:
2 cups milk
6 tbs. sugar
½ cup all-purpose flour
3 egg yolks
1 tb. finely chopped mixed candied
   peel

FOR THE MERINGUE:
3 egg whites
½ cup sugar

FOR THE DECORATION:
strips of candied orange peel
sugar

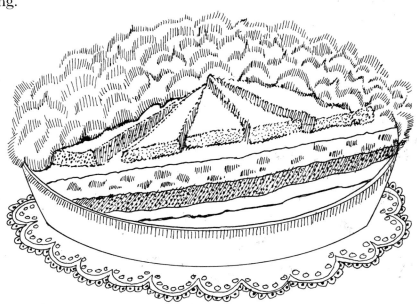

cross section of trifle

St. Joseph's Fritters

BIGNÈ DI SAN GIUSEPPE

Serves 6

6 tbs. butter
1 cup cold water
1½ cups all-purpose flour
4 eggs
2 egg yolks
1 tsp. sugar
2 tsps. grated lemon rind
olive oil and lard for deep-frying
vanilla sugar

To make vanilla sugar, cut a whole vanilla bean crosswise into 3 equal parts. Then cut each piece in half lengthwise and with the point of a small knife, loosen the central seeds in each half. Bury the pieces in 2 pounds of sugar. Keep the jar tightly closed for one week and the sugar will be permeated with vanilla flavor. As the sugar is used, add more to the jar. The bean will give off flavor for 6 to 9 months.

St. Joseph's Day is celebrated in Italy with much feasting, since he is the patron saint of hearth and home. This is one of the many dishes which have become specialties for this saint's day.

Place the butter, a pinch of salt, and the water in a saucepan. Over low heat, bring to a boil. Remove from the heat and, all at once, add the flour. Blend together thoroughly with a wooden spoon, then replace over the heat, and stir until the paste comes away from the side of the pan to form a ball. When this begins to sizzle, remove from the heat, allow to cool slightly, and then beat in the eggs and egg yolks one at a time, beating thoroughly after each addition.

When tiny bubbles appear, add the sugar and lemon rind and mix until thoroughly blended. Form into a ball, remove from the pan, and let stand, wrapped in a cloth, in a cool place for about 30 minutes.

Roll pieces of the dough into walnut-sized balls. Heat the olive oil and lard in a large saucepan over moderate heat and drop in several of the balls. The puffs will turn over automatically in the hot oil. When they begin to swell, increase the heat. Fry for about 5 to 10 minutes, or until golden brown; then remove and drain. Let the oil cool slightly; then repeat the procedure with several more balls. It is best to fry only a few puffs at a time. Arrange on a serving plate covered with a paper napkin and sprinkle with vanilla sugar. Serve very hot.

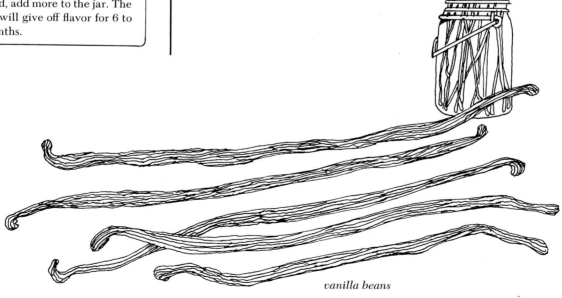

vanilla beans

Menu Planning and Wine Guide

Menu planning, like any other homemaking task, should be done with as much pertinent information on hand as is possible. Circumstances will dictate the bounds within which the homemaker must work. A family meal may not feature as lavish a main dish as one served for guests. Or the antipasto may not be as widely varied for one meal as for another. Many times an antipasto plate of celery, radishes, beets, and anchovies, banked with a green and white lettuce border will be quickly assembled by a rushed housewife. At another, less hurried time, she will prepare a platter full of prosciutto, tomatoes, olives, marinated artichoke hearts, stuffed hard-boiled eggs, mushroom caps with gorgonzola, or any other of an endless variety of hot and cold appetizers.

To plan and prepare an authentic Italian meal you must consider the dishes to be prepared and then examine them in relation to the whole meal. A multicourse meal should be an artful blend of flavors and textures, never sharp or overly spiced, and never repetitious. The Italian housewife would never serve two pasta courses at the same meal, nor would she serve a fish soup and then a baked fish entrée. Each course is prepared with pride and must be in harmony with the other dishes.

Wine is a staple in most Italian households and you'll find that there is a wine for almost every course—a vermouth or chilled white wine with the antipasto, a mild wine with the entrée, a sweet wine with dessert, and a liqueur with or after coffee. As you plan your menu, give thought and care to the selection of wines you will serve. And remember, the quality of wine used in cooking must be equal to the table wine because when the alcohol evaporates, as it does in cooking, the only trace of the wine that is left is the flavor. If you have used an inferior or so-called cooking wine, you will be left with a poor quality taste in your food. It is important to remember that wine is used to heighten the character of certain dishes. It should not be used indiscriminately, but only where the recipe calls for it and only as much as is called for.

Italian wines are modest compared to French wines, with only a few vintage years. Chianti is perhaps the most well-known red wine in the world. It is a dry, light wine of highly variable quality. The very best are the Classicos from the inner district of the Chianti region. The bottle of a Chianti Classico usually carries a neck band depicting a young rooster in black on a gold background with a red border. Chianti Classico *Vecchio*

(old) has been aged in cask and bottle for at least two years. Chianti Classico *Riserva* has been aged for at least three years. Some of the truly great
Riservas are aged in wood for over three years and in the bottle for another five. They are magnificent wines by any standards.

The best red wines of Italy, after the great Chianti Classicos, come
from the Piedmont region. And the best of these are made in and around
the village of Barolo, just south of Alba, from the Nebbiolo grape. Some
of this wine is aged in casks for more than five years before being bottled.

Valpolicella and Bardolino are two other dry red Italian wines. They
are almost as famous as Chianti and are extremely enjoyable, being fresh
and light-bodied.

Soave, Verdicchio, Frascati, and Orvieto are all white wines. Soave
is a pale, dry white wine that is drunk quite young—two or three years
after vintage. Verdicchio and Frascati are both dry wines, while Orvieto,
which has more character than most white wines, can be either dry
(*secco*) or sweet (*abboccato*).

No hard and fast rules apply to which wine should be drunk with
which food. You should choose a wine that pleases you and complements
the food you are serving. Should you feel uncertain, the following guide
will help you make your selection.

Antipasto: sweet or dry vermouth.
Fish and shellfish: a dry or medium dry white or a light red wine.
Pasta: light or heavy red wine.
Red meat and game: light or heavy red wine.
White meat and fowl: a dry white or light red wine.
Dessert: sweet white or red wine or Marsala.
Coffee and after dinner: anisette, brandy, Strega, grappa.

Asti Spumante, called the champagne of Italian wines, can be served, as
French champagne is served, throughout a meal. It is a light, sparkling
wine and goes with any dish. It should always be served well chilled.

As you become more familiar with the tastes and types of wines you
will no doubt want to start experimenting and will find there is as much
leeway in serving wines as there are individual tastes.

Remember also that wines need not be imported to be given your
consideration. Some of the finest wines in the world are produced in the
vineyards of California and New York and many connoisseurs include
them in their choice of worthy vintages.

When you find a wine that pleases you it is wise to buy several
bottles from your dealer. He may have purchased that vineyard's entire
supply and your chances of finding it again, once his stock is depleted,
will be slim. He will be happy to give you all the information you need on
how to store it so the last bottle will be as good as the first.

On the following pages are a listing of typical Italian luncheon and
dinner menus which we offer as a guide. Once you have become familiar
with the limitless varieties of Italian foods, you will surely let your imagination take flight and create many, many more.

POTATO DUMPLINGS WITH CHEESE
BRAISED BEEF
GREEN SALAD
FRUIT SALAD
Chianti Classico

&

PARMA HAM WITH FIGS
BRAISED VEAL SHANKS
MILANESE RICE
FRESH PARMESAN CHEESE AND FRUIT
Bardolino

&

SPAGHETTI WITH BACON, EGG, AND CHEESE
SWEETBREADS IN MARSALA AND MEAT SAUCE
MIXED GREEN SALAD
SICILIAN PASTRY HORNS
Orvieto Rosé

&

DEEP-FRIED OPEN CHEESE SANDWICH
LAMB FRICASSEE
LETTUCE SALAD
FRUIT
Lake Garda Rosé

&

COLD EGGPLANT APPETIZER
LAMB STEW
ST. JOSEPH'S FRITTERS
Barbaresco

STUFFED PASTA WITH WALNUT SAUCE
FRIED LIVER AND SWEETBREADS
DEEP-FRIED ARTICHOKE HEARTS
MARSALA CUSTARD
Verdicchio

&

ANCHOVY OMELET
VENETIAN BEEF STEW WITH POLENTA
TOMATO SALAD
FRUIT
Valpolicella

&

RIBBON NOODLES WITH RICOTTA CHEESE
MIXED FRIED FISH
PEPPER AND TOMATO STEW
FRUIT
Soave

&

TOMATO AND ANCHOVY PIZZA
MUSSEL HOT POT
TOMATO SALAD
FRUIT
Frascati

&

MUSSELS WITH WHITE WINE AND GARLIC
STEAK WITH TOMATO AND GARLIC
MIXED GREEN SALAD
FRUIT
Chianti

CLAM SOUP
FLORENTINE GRILLED STEAKS
BEANS IN A FLASK
FRUIT SALAD
Barolo

❧

CHICKEN BOUILLON WITH POACHED EGGS
MILANESE VEAL CHOPS
GREEN SALAD
DEEP-FRIED PASTRIES
FRUIT
Verdicchio

❧

CHEESE-STUFFED PASTA IN BOUILLON
GRILLED LIVER
STUFFED TOMATOES
FRUIT
Valpolicella

❧

RICE AND SHELLFISH SALAD
BRAISED DUCK WITH TURNIPS
STRAWBERRIES WITH LEMON JUICE
Soave

❧

VERMICELLI WITH TOMATO SAUCE
VEAL WITH HAM AND SAGE
SLICED FRIED MUSHROOMS
TRIFLE
Verdicchio

VEGETABLE AND PASTA SOUP
DEEP-FRIED VEAL AND SAUSAGE
DEEP-FRIED ARTICHOKE HEARTS
TRIFLE
Chianti

❧

FAVA BEAN SOUP
TURKEY WITH CHESTNUT STUFFING
GREEN SALAD
GORGONZOLA CHEESE AND FRUIT
Bardolino

❧

CHICKEN RISOTTO
FRIED SHRIMP
MIXED GREEN SALAD
BEL PAESE CHEESE AND FRUIT
Orvieto

❧

BEEF BOUILLON WITH DUMPLINGS
GARNISHED CHILLED SOLE
TOMATO SALAD
FRESH PARMESAN CHEESE AND FRUIT
Frascati

❧

MUSSELS WITH WHITE WINE AND GARLIC
STEWED GOOSE
PEPPER AND TOMATO STEW
FONTINA CHEESE WITH FRUIT
Bardolino

Guide to Dining Out

A first-time visitor to Italy may be confused by the abundance of eating and drinking establishments that he will encounter and wonder which is the most appropriate to his needs and budget.

The best dining in Italy is not necessarily the most expensive. There are countless little restaurants, some well known and others off the beaten track, that vary in price from medium to delightfully inexpensive. Hunting out their locations and sampling their specialties can often be one of the highlights of a trip.

If you haven't Christopher Columbus's instinct for discovery, however, there are any number of well-publicized restaurants that welcome the hungry traveller and whose waiters are sympathetic to the hazards presented by an unfamiliar menu. The staffs of these restaurants often speak some English, and are generally quite friendly. They will be happy to suggest dishes suitable to your taste and, at your request, will warn you against those dishes that are for the more sophisticated palate.

It is standard practice in Italy for the restaurants to display a menu in the window. This will give you the pertinent information you will need before you venture inside to try the food. It will tell you prices for complete meals and à la carte dishes, and whether or not wine is included in the price of the meal. If there is a cover charge, that will be listed as well.

Normally a service charge or tip of 15% will be added to the bill before it is presented to you. However, if the service has been exceptionally good and the waiter extra patient with your faltering Italian, another 2 or 3% may be added, but this is absolutely a matter of choice. If the service charge is not included on the bill, you must add the 15% in the same way you would tip a waiter at home.

You must also be prepared for the sales tax on all food and drink.

Breakfast in Italy will be light, usually only coffee with milk, tea, or hot chocolate; fresh bread or a roll served with a choice of jam or marmalade. Because Italians begin the day with a snack, lunch and dinner are the main meals and the Italians firmly believe in multicourse dining. This is not to say that they overeat. To the contrary, the meals are usually well balanced and the menu will contain various types of hors d'oeuvres, an antipasto plate, soup or a dry entrée, meat or fish accompanied by one or more vegetables, then cheese and fruit or a sweet dessert and coffee. Naturally the quality and variety of the food will depend upon the region you are in and the type of restaurant you have chosen. Generally you can expect the food to be good and the portions generous.

Listed below is a description of the various types of Italian restaurants and the kinds of meals they serve.

Italian Name	*Description*
Trattoria	A restaurant that serves simple food and drink; medium priced.
Taverna	Like a trattoria, but usually less expensive.
Buca	Small restaurant, with limited but often excellent menu.
Locale Notturno	A nightclub; though not fancy, rather expensive.
Osteria	An inn where simple food and wine is served.
Caffee-bar	Primarily a drinking establishment. Some serve breakfast and snacks.
Ristorante	Restaurants are classified by the standard of the cuisine and service. Prices vary accordingly.
Autogrill	A large highway restaurant; waiter and/or self-service.
Tavola Calda	A snackbar.

The Italians consider wine the perfect accompaniment to a meal and don't consider any table correctly set unless it includes a bottle or two of the local vintage. Except for Chiantis, very little Italian wine is shipped from province to province, so the wines you order will be local ones. When the wine is brought to your table, but before it is uncorked, inspect the label to make sure that it is the wine you ordered. After it has been opened, see that the cork is in one piece and does not smell sour. You taste the wine to find out if it is good. The only reasons you should ever return a wine are if it has turned sour or contains sediment.

To familiarize you with traditional menus of restaurants in Italy, the following pages show a menu from a typically small classic restaurant serving food *a lá casalinga,* and another from a more formal restaurant serving food *di riguardo.*

Menù Italiano di Riguardo

MINESTRA (soups)

BRODO DI MANZO
beef broth

STRACCIATELLE
consomme with egg

MINESTRONE
bean soup

ANTIPASTI (appetizers)

MELONE CON PROSCIUTTO
melon with ham

FUNGHI CON ACETO E OLIO
*sauteed cold mushrooms
marinated in salad dressing*

SEDANI
celery hearts

CARCIOFINI
artichoke hearts

VONGOLI AL FORNO
baked clams

PASTA (noodles)

RAVIOLI ALL'INGLESE
ravioli with butter and parmesan cheese

RISOTTO ALLA MILANESE
rice with saffron

SPAGHETTI CON SALSA DI VONGOLI
spaghetti with clam sauce

LASAGNA AL FORNO
baked noodles

FETTUCCINE VERDI CON LE ERBE
green noodles with basil

PESCE (fish)

SPADA AL VINO BIANCO
swordfish in white wine

ARAGOSTA OREGANATA
lobster with oregano

SGOMBRO RIPIENO
*mackeral stuffed with
cheese and mushrooms*

ENTRÉES (main courses)

FEGATO CON VINO
liver with claret

LA BISTECCA FIORENTINA
Florentine steak

POLLO CON MARSALA
chicken with Marsala

VITELLO ROLE DI PARMA
veal roll with prosciutto ham

PERNICE AL FORNO
roasted partridge

LEGUMI (vegetables)

ESCAROLE SAUTÉ
sautéed escarole

FAGIOLINI AL GROVIERA
green beans with cheese

FUNGHI ALLA PARMESAN
mushrooms with parmesan cheese

ZUCCHINI DOLCE E AGRO
sweet and sour squash

MELANZANA ALLA GRIGLIA
eggplant grilled with cheese

INSALATA (salads)

INSALATA DI POMODORO CON OREGANO
tomatoes with oregano dressing

INSALATA MISTI
mixed green salad

INSALATA DI FINOCCHIO
fennel salad

INSALATA DI ZUCCHINI
zucchini salad

FORMAGGI (cheeses)

BEL PAESE, FONTINA, GORGONZOLA, MANTECA, MASCARPONE, STRACCHINO

DOLCI (desserts)

PESCA CON VINO ROSSO
peach with brandy

ZUPPA INGLESE
rum cake with custard

SPUMONI
ice cream

MELONE
melon

ZABAGLIONE
Marsala custard

Menù Italiano Casalingo

MINESTRA *(soups)*

ZUPPA DI LENTICCHI
lentil soup

ZUPPA DI PESCE
fish soup

MINESTRONE
bean soup

ANTIPASTI *(appetizers)*

CARCIOFINI
artichoke hearts

VUNGOLI AL FORNO
baked clams

CAPOCOLLO
smoked pork sliced thin

PEPERONCINI ALL'ACETO
green peppers pickled in vinegar

PIMENTO
sweet red pepper

UOVO DI TONNO
tuna fish roe

PASTA *(noodles)*

POLENTA CON SALSICCIA
corn meal pudding with sausage

LASAGNA IMBOTTITE
stuffed noodles

RIGATONI CON SALSICCIA
rigatoni with sausage

SPAGHETTI CON ACCIUGHE
spaghetti with anchovies

TORTA CON DITALI
macaroni, meat, and cheese pie

PIZZA CON SALSICCIA
pizza with sausage

ENTRÉES *(main courses)*

SGOMBRO RIPIENO
mackerel stuffed with cheese and mushrooms

VONGOLI SICILIANA
steamed clams Sicilian

POLPETTONE CON RICOTTA
meat loaf with ricotta cheese

FILETTO SICILIANA
filet mignon Sicilian-style

UMIDO DI CARNE
beef and lamb stew

SALSICCIA ALLA GRIGLIA
broiled sausage

COSTATELLE DI MAILLE CON CAVOLO
pork chops and cabbage

FRITTATA DI CARNE E VEGETALI
vegetable and meat omelet

LEGUMI *(vegetables)*

STUFATINO DI CARCIOFI
braised artichokes

BROCCOLI CON OLIVE
broccoli with olives

CAVOLO IMBOTTITO
stuffed cabbage

PEPERONI ARROSTITI
roasted peppers

MELANZANA FRITTA
fried eggplant

SPINACI AFFOGATI
steamed spinach

INSALATA *(salads)*

INSALATA DI CICORIA FINA
dandelion salad

INSALATA DI PATATE E UOVO
potato and egg salad

INSALATA DI FINOCCHIO,
POMODORO, E CICORIA
fennel, tomato, and chicory salad

INSALATA D'ARANCIO E LIMONE
orange and lemon salad

INSALATA DI CALAMAI
squid salad

FORMAGGI *(cheeses)*

PARMIGIANO, GORGONZOLA, STRACCHINO, PROVOLONE

DOLCI *(desserts)*

TORTA DI RICOTTA
Italian cheese pie

GRANITA DI LIMONE
lemon ice

TORTA DI MANDORLE
almond cake

Index

Those entries which appear in SMALL CAPITAL LETTERS are the Italian recipe titles. Roman numbers refer to recipes, *italic numbers* to the text.

Illustrations and Photographs